52

WAYS TO IGNITE
YOUR CONGREGATION . . .

BIBLE STUDY

BARBARA J. ESSEX

THE
PILGRIM
PRESS
Cleveland

The Pilgrim Press
700 Prospect Avenue
Cleveland, Ohio 44115
thepilgrimpress.com

Library of Congress Cataloging-in-Publication Data

Essex, Barbara J. (Barbara Jean),1951–
    52 ways to ignite your congregation– : Bible study / Barbara J. Essex
      p.   cm.
    ISBN 978-0-8298-1876-5 (alk. paper)
    1. Bible – Study and teaching. 2. Bible – Hermeneutics. I. Title.
BS600.3.E87 2012
220.071 – dc23   2012014276

Contents

Introduction

My relationship with the Bible began when I was about ten years old. I wanted to know more about the book that sat on the coffee table in our living room. Our family Bible was a big white leather-bound book. My mother admonished us not to touch it—the book was too important for our grubby hands. The only time I ever touched that Bible was to move it so I could dust the table. I saw my mother write updates in the Family section of the Bible, but I never saw anyone in our home actually read it. Despite the obvious importance of the book, we knew the Bible was not a book to be handled. But I was curious.

I confess that I was disappointed when I finally worked up the nerve to open the pages of our family Bible. The language was strange and difficult to understand. It would be a while before I learned about King James and his version of the Bible. But the die had been cast—the Bible was too bulky, too strangely written to appeal to me. Even more than the size and language, I couldn't make any connections among the various parts of the Bible. There were contradictory creation stories and unexplained, illogical events. The Psalms were beautiful but who could make sense of Proverbs? The Gospels were compelling dramas but the Epistles seemed incomplete. And what on earth was going on in Revelation?

I gave up on the Bible. Needless to say, worship for me was "interesting." I loved church music and the prayers. The various liturgies were moving and helped deepen my faith. The sense of community I felt at church kept me engaged. More often than not, though, the sermons didn't really move me. Then, something happened the summer I turned thirteen. I used to spend the summers with my maternal grandparents in Birmingham, Alabama. Each July, their church sponsored a revival week— a time of singing, praying, and preaching with the intent of "bringing the unsaved to Jesus." Those who had not confessed Jesus as their personal savior had to sit on the front pew, also called the moaners' bench. In many ways, the preacher directed his (and it was always "his" back in those days) sermon directly to the unsaved. That particular summer, the preacher was a brilliant storyteller: he portrayed such a human Jesus that I fully expected Jesus to walk the aisle that very night. I had not heard a sermon that brought Jesus into the twentieth century and I became a believer. The preacher painted a picture from the Bible that rekindled my interest. The quest to understand the Bible resumed. I remained stumped by much of what I read, but I kept at it, with uneven results.

Some years later, I was invited to attend worship at Trinity United Church of Christ on Chicago's Southside. The first time I heard the Rev. Jeremiah A. Wright, Jr., preach, I had a flashback to the preaching I heard in that small church in Birmingham—brilliant storytelling with real life connections. Rev. Wright set the stage for exploring the biblical text: providing background information and relating the text to contemporary and current events. The personalities and situations in the Bible were expertly connected to what was happening in our world and time. I was helped by having information about the context of the scripture and some sense of how the texts came to be. A different phase of my journey began. I confess, though, that I ventured into my first Bible study class out of guilt. Every Sunday Rev. Wright talked about "so-called" Christians who didn't know the Bible. He was clear that we ought not take his words about the Bible uncritically. We had the privilege of reading and studying the Bible for ourselves, and we needed to take advantage of the opportunity. And it seemed that he was always looking at me when he said these things. Of course he wasn't, but it was enough to get me out of my comfort zone and into a Bible study class. Not only did the class change my life, it spawned a ministry and mission—making the Bible fun for everyone. Bible study is now a way of life for me.

52 Ways to Ignite Your Congregation—Bible Study is a contribution to The Pilgrim Press's series to help breathe new life into congregations. This volume offers ways to spark interest in Bible study by getting people excited about reading and studying the Bible and applying its principles to their real and everyday lives.

Many people are intimidated by the Bible, although the Christian faith is rooted and grounded in the sacred texts. This book is designed to alleviate the anxiety, fear, and discomfort that persons feel when approaching the Bible. This book offers easy and practical, hands-on, how-to approaches to Bible study.

My interest in the Bible was piqued by a minister who preached the Bible so vividly that I was able to put myself into the stories and feel what the biblical characters must have felt. The Bible came alive and the richness was exposed in ways that helped me think about my life and choices from a theological perspective. The Bible is the most fascinating book ever written. No wonder it continues to be a bestseller thousands of years later. I hope you will find the Bible to be an exciting, energizing, life-giving book.

52 Ways to Ignite Your Congregation—Bible Study is divided into two sections:

1. The Nuts and Bolts: Administrative Hints

2. The Good Stuff: Methods and Strategies

The "ways" are short and practical. You can start to implement them right away. Some overlap and build on each other. Some are stand-alone hints. Almost all of the fifty-two ways grow out of my experience as pastor and teacher. Although a good part of my ministry has been in seminary settings, I have always maintained close ties to a variety of diverse congregations—preaching and teaching and getting feedback on what works and what doesn't. I'm grateful for this opportunity to share my learnings with you.

The bottom line is this: the Bible is many things to many people. We are to be mindful of the various contexts of the biblical record, and we should be mindful of the various contexts in which we study it. The Bible, at the very least, is the record of our ancestors' relationship to and with God—and points to the possibilities we have with this same God.

The Bible tells us about a God who loves us and saves us by God's grace despite who we are or what we do. The Bible is a witness that contains stories of triumph, trials, troubles, failures, and victories. The Bible is a witness to a God who is and creates, a Christ who cares and redeems, and a Spirit who comforts and guides.

Bible study helps us gain glimpses into who God is and how God deals with us. Further, Bible study helps us see ourselves more clearly in light of God's gracious and merciful dealings with us. May you find time to study God's Word, and may you be blessed by what you learn and by what confronts and challenges you!

Part I

THE NUTS AND BOLTS: ADMINISTRATIVE HINTS

I've heard pastors and pastors-in-training complain about Bible study. They often don't know where to start. Or they don't know how to "translate" their seminary learnings into classes for lay-persons. I understand the dilemma. So here are some hints on how to get that Bible study going.

1

Spark Interest in
Knowing the Bible

Nothing will happen until and unless people have an interest in knowing the Bible. This is essential. If want to ignite your congregation, get them excited about studying God's Word.

Many pastors do not teach the Bible! As surprising as this may sound, it carries some truth. For some, the Bible is too hard to teach, even when one has studied it in seminary. In fact, seminary education may make the Bible too difficult to tackle in any substantive way. The historical-critical method certainly raises more questions than it provides answers. By the time a pastor explains form criticism, literary criticism, source criticism, textual criticism, and redaction criticism—everyone's heads will be aching and spinning. A pastor will likely see eyes glaze over when attempting to explain the various traditions that comprise the Hebrew Bible (and what happened to calling the first part of the Bible the "Old Testament"?). There is the *Yahwist,* actually called "J"; *Elohist* for "Elohim," the Hebrew plural for God; *Priestly;* and just what is *"D?"* Is it Deuteronomic, Deuteronomist, or Deuteronomistic? And just how does one explain rhetorical criticism, the historicity of Jesus—you see what I mean? It's simply easier to preach and hope that folks can connect the dots. But the problem is, most folks don't get it, at least not without substantial help.

Pastors are called to the ministry of Word and Sacrament—preaching, teaching, and administering the sacraments. The fact that so many shy away from the teaching aspect is telling. It's not, I believe, that pastors are slackers or intentionally try to shirk their duties. Rather, I think many are overwhelmed by the task. How does one take all the biblical scholarship available and make it accessible to the person sitting in the pew? This is no small task and there are few courses offered in seminary on the art of teaching. Add to that the pace at which seminary biblical courses run and one's own grappling with how to connect scholarship with faith—it's a wonder we complete seminary at all.

I suggest that you start from the simple fact that the Bible is a collection of stories, poems, and object lessons. I mean, really, who doesn't enjoy a good story? Want family drama? Murder and mayhem? International espionage and cold war tactics? Love stories of every kind? Far from being a boring read, the Bible is filled with interesting characters, life-changing scenarios, sticky situations, and unpredictable outcomes.

Many in our congregations can relate to the many situations and circumstances we find in the Bible: marital discord (Adam and Eve); misplaced maternal affection (Rebecca and Jacob); unrequited love (Hosea and Gomer); an innocent man wrongly accused and executed for a crime he did not commit (Jesus). Are these plots for new reality shows on television? Not even close. All of these are biblical stories and situations. There are a multitude of areas to explore—war, incest, domestic violence, exploitation of the poor, subversive use of power and influence, romance, intrigue, espionage—there is something for everyone and more. In the Bible, we learn more about who God is and who God is calling us to be. In the Bible, we learn more about ourselves through the stories of men and women who behave too much like us. Yet God loves them and uses them to a greater glory. In the Bible, we learn about love, grace, forgiveness, second chances, and redeemed choices. It is important to kindle an interest in knowing the Bible, the story of our God and God's dealings with humanity.

The fact is that Bible study requires time and commitment. There's no way around that. Of course, there are tools to make the teaching task easier. But before anything else, you must exude genuine excitement, interest, and enthusiasm for the Bible. If you aren't excited about the Bible, how can you expect the congregation to be? You can usher folks into a different world—strange, confusing, frustrating—just like real life! And all the while, you are helping people to see God, our God who beckons us into relationship, all in the midst of real challenges, triumphs, trials, false starts, and victories. We get to see a God who strengthens and nurtures us along life's journey, surrounding us with love, grace, and mercy. Who can resist this pull? Get folks excited about the possibilities of encountering this God and deepening that relationship. The first step in igniting your congregation through Bible study? Generate interest and excitement in knowing the Bible!

2

Invite the Holy Spirit
into the Process

We can be proficient in planning and charting a course, but
there will be no life until and unless we invite the Holy Spirit to
direct our intentions and to bless our work. We invite the Holy
Spirit through prayer, meditation, and listening. When we are
open and receptive, the Holy Spirit empowers and guides our
thinking. Pray for guidance as you unfold a plan for Bible study;
ask God what the plan should be. You may be surprised at how
quickly direction comes when you are still, open, and listening.
Yes, you must listen to what God says in response to your plan.
Remember that the hope for Bible study is not to reap accolades
for yourself but to empower people to work on their relationship with God.

People come to every gathering of the church with their
own set of issues, concerns, hurts, and embarrassments. We all
have baggage and we bring it into every setting we enter. And
wouldn't you know that folks bring their baggage to Bible study.
For many persons, Bible study class takes them back to their
elementary or high school days—days filled with boring classes,
insane amounts of homework, and less than stellar grades. Any
learning situation can take us back to unpleasant times. All the
more important that we take some time to pray and ask for the
Holy Spirit's help.

Some may have had great Bible study experiences; their
expectations are high that your courses will meet the stan-
dards set by previous explorations. Some have had awful experiences around Bible study. The teacher may not have put in
adequate time for preparation. Or the teacher was not effective

in conveying information. Or the class was more like a seminary class than a Bible study. Perhaps the class was not organized well, or it wasn't clear what the aims of the class were. Some may have been made to feel embarrassed by the teacher or other students for asking what seemed like a reasonable question.

Pray that the Spirit opens the hearts and minds of the people who will be teaching *and* those who will be studying the Bible. Pray that the Spirit will calm the fears that people bring with them to Bible study. Some will be skeptical, some will be downright scared, and others will be intimidated. Ask the Spirit to infuse a sense of peace before, during, and after the class.

Bible study should be an adventure, not a walk toward despair. The unknown is scary: the Spirit is always assuring us with words of comfort: Fear not! Do not underestimate the presence of the Holy Spirit in any setting where God's Word is being explored. Only in this way can we expect transformation—change hearts and lives.

In today's fast-paced and ever-changing culture, we don't spend much time tarrying with the Holy Spirit. We barely mention the Spirit in worship, let alone invite the Spirit's power into our midst. Don't make this mistake when it comes to Bible study. Students will be introduced to new ideas and concepts, many of which will seem to undermine faith rather than support it. By being mindful of God's Spirit, people will be more receptive to learning new things that will not cause them to turn from their faith. As persons get more and more involved in Bible study, you will notice a marked changed in the ways persons relate to each other and to the work of the church. Because people have prayed and studied together, you will notice much more harmony and cooperation, and this is another benefit of corporate Bible study: meaningful exchanges, fellowship, and deeper discipleship.

③

Create a Working Bible Study Curriculum

Don't be intimidated by this statement. Although it sounds so academic, it is important to think about what you want to accomplish, with God's help. What I'm asking you to do, after much prayer and meditation and listening, is to develop an overall plan for Bible study. What do you want to do first, second, third, and so on?

A curriculum outlines a set of courses for a Bible study program. A curriculum is different from a course syllabus: the curriculum is the big picture and the syllabi represent the details of each class. The curriculum will define the general goal for the program; for example, one goal might be that at the end of a particular number of classes, the student will be able to name all the books of the Bible and provide a short overview or summary of each. Another goal might be that students are able to provide short biographies of a set list of biblical names. Another goal might be that students are able to articulate the theological underpinnings of baptism and communion. Whatever your goals, you will design courses to assist students to achieve them.

At the curriculum level, you will determine the order in which courses should be taken, which require prerequisites and which are advanced courses, and the length of each class. It is important to have a mix of some shorter (say, four weeks) and longer (up to 12 weeks or longer) courses. For instance, in the curriculum for my congregation, students had to complete a four-week Bible Basics course before they could move on to other courses. It is helpful for the entire congregation to know the Bible Study curriculum so they will get a sense of the overall plan.

Spend some time thinking about your congregation and how you want to approach Bible study. This becomes your vision for faith formation. Realize, too, that you don't have to do this all by yourself. You might consider convening a small task force to help you think about how to approach an overall plan for education in your church, which might include some general thinking of what offerings there need to be for children, youth, young adults, adults, and older adults. The task force can brainstorm ideas for each age group as well as the venue—Sunday School, Youth Ministry, Adult Bible Study, and so forth. The point is that some thought is given to the educational program for the church, including Bible study.

It doesn't take folks long to realize when there is no plan and that you are winging it. They will quickly lose interest because they have no sense of where they are headed. We can take a lesson from Moses as he led the Hebrews out of Egypt with no clear vision of where they were going. It was easier, then, for folks to become discouraged and they longed for Egypt, not because they liked being oppressed but rather because it was familiar. They knew what to expect. In the wilderness, they had no idea of what was on the horizon. In the face of an unarticulated destination, the people became angry and fearful. This is not a good way to approach Bible study. A plan is in order.

Folks want to know where things are leading and that the plan makes sense. My approach was a fairly simple one: start slowly and progress to the more difficult areas once people felt more secure about learning. Even a simple curriculum is better than none at all. A curriculum can be modified, but it is better to start with a tentative chart of study.

4

Choose the Right Day and Time

A pastor once lamented to me that people were not showing up for Bible study on Wednesday nights. It was the one night of the week when there were no church meetings scheduled. He was pastor of a small suburban church. Nearly all of the members lived in other neighborhoods and commuted each Sunday for church and for various meetings. The pastor thought a weeknight would be ideal because it would not interfere with work schedules or other church meetings.

He was excited about the Wednesday night Bible Study class and prepared his lessons carefully. He allowed ample time to publicize the class and tried his best to generate excitement about this new opportunity at the church. The first week drew ten people. The pastor was excited and felt that the class would grow in time. The next week, seven people attended. The pastor, a bit disappointed, still rejoiced that he had a good group of folk for the class. The third week four people showed up for the class. The fourth week no one showed up for the class. The pastor wondered what he was doing wrong that kept people from attending Bible study. He prepared the lessons and the space for the next two Wednesdays and no one showed up for either. He was stumped! He felt he had done all the right things and he was always prepared to teach, but no one came.

When I asked if he had talked to those who attended early on about why they had stopped attending, he admitted that he had not had a conversation with them. As simple as it seemed, I suggested he just ask them. When he finally polled the congregation, he discovered that most of his members were older and fearful of driving at night. He moved the Bible study to

Sunday after worship and included a potluck lunch. The Bible study thrived because he chose the right day and time for study. Determine the times when folks are most likely to attend Bible study classes and set your classes to accommodate the attendees. Consider all the possibilities—should there be day classes for those who work at night? Should there be weekend classes for those who work overtime during the week? Should there be morning classes? You will need to know your congregation in order to answer these questions. Be flexible and do your best to accommodate people's lives in providing educational opportunities.

5

Offer a Variety of Days and Times for Bible Study

There may not be any one day or time that will work for your congregation. It is important to offer as many classes as you can so people have options. Not everyone is available on Wednesday evenings at 7:00 p.m. You may have persons in the congregation who work nights or have care-giver responsibilities in the evenings. And busy parents may have all kinds of activities planned for their children during the week and on the weekends. Therefore, you should offer classes during the day and on weekends.

Flexible time offerings will go a long way in igniting your congregation around Bible study. The variety of offerings will signal to the congregation that Bible study is so important that there are many options from which to choose. Offering courses at different times also encourages members to become teachers and to provide leadership for Bible studies.

Don't let time constraints become an excuse for persons not to study God's Word. Set days and times for Bible study so that they are as convenient for your members as possible. My home church in Cleveland offers classes on Saturday mornings at 8:00 a.m., Friday evenings at 7:00 p.m., Wednesday mornings at 10:00 a.m., Wednesday evenings at 7:00 p.m., and Sunday mornings at 9:00 a.m. The possibilities are abundant and people will be grateful and blessed to have options for Bible study.

6

Know Your Student

It is important to have a sense of who your student is. There are some things we know about adult learners that can be helpful in creating a Bible study program for them. It is important to assure adults that Bible study will be a safe place. For some adults, the classroom is a threatening place. They feel they might fail or be ridiculed for not knowing what they think they should. Some are embarrassed about what they don't know.

All adults bring a wealth of experience to their study of the Bible. They may downplay what they know or they might not believe that they know anything that will enhance their study of the Bible. But they should be respected for the wisdom they have already.

Adults learn best when there is a sense of community. Some will protest that they prefer to study alone, and this might be true for them. Their choice may not really reflect how they learn. The excuses may be covers for insecurity and anxiety about being in a classroom setting. Once people have experienced fun and informative Bible study, they quickly overcome their hesitancy. I have found that providing a safe and open space allows students to engage the material and each other in profound and life-changing ways. For Christians, the norm is community. This is countercultural to "American" rugged individualism. We need each other for support and to learn in effective ways. We relate to the Bible by exploring relationships—with the text and within the context of church and community.

Adults learn effectively when they are encouraged to collaborate. This, of course, flies in the face of traditional schooling where students are in competition with each other. Bible study is a good place for people to work together to achieve an end. This need for connection is perfect for small group activities and group discussion. Learning to work together transfers to all areas of life, not just Bible study. Your congregation will be ignited when folks understand their commonalities, commit themselves to the same goal, and volunteer to share their gifts with the church. A sense of community and camaraderie will be part of the foundation of good church life. And this can start in Bible study!

7

Establish a Process
for Conversation

If members don't know each other well, you may want to enlist
the help of the class to create a set of guidelines for the Bible
study. You want people to feel safe and free to speak their minds.
A process for conversation might be just what is needed to get
people to participate fully. Suggested guidelines include:

- Understand that the only dumb question is the one not
  asked; all questions are valid;
- Exercise no judgment; everyone's opinions and feelings
  are legitimate;
- Respect each other;
- Respect silence; don't feel pressured to speak; we learn
  from listening *and* speaking;
- Actively listen to each other; pay attention to what others
  are saying;
- Use "I" statements and speak only for yourself; let others
  speak for themselves;
- Share only what is comfortable for you;
- What happens in Bible study stays in Bible study! Respect
  confidentiality;
- Overparticipation and underparticipation are equally det-
  rimental to effective learning.

Let the group determine the ground rules for engagement.
You may want to post the rules someplace in the space as a
reminder. Or provide copies to every member. If the conversation gets heated, go back to the ground rules. This will ensure
that persons feel safe in the space.

8

Encourage Persons to Make a Commitment to Study the Bible

It is important once interest is piqued that persons make a commitment to study the Bible. The Bible, the world's bestseller, is also quite a difficult book to read and understand. The Bible requires us to feel something as we read and study it.

Invite persons to make a solid commitment to stay the course. By making Bible study fun, you will help persons stay engaged in the study. The Bible will bring up feelings and reactions, some of which have nothing to do with the Bible itself but will be some unresolved issue or concern. While Bible study is not intended to be therapeutic, there may be cause to address particular issues and concerns.

Have information handy in case you need to make referrals for issues that cannot be addressed in Bible study or in consultation with the pastor. Don't be intimidated by the concerns that people bring with them to class. The religious enterprise can be life-changing, and Bible study is sure to bring up complex feelings. Be prepared to assist in healthy ways.

9

Start with the Basics

I was surprised to hear one of my church members remark that she had been a member of the church her entire life, but she didn't know anything about the Bible. Well, she overstated the point, but I understood what she was saying. The Bible is an intimidating book. My own history with the Bible bears this out. As I mentioned above our family Bible was big and bulky, and occupied a special place on our living room coffee table. We were admonished about mishandling this important book.

I still remember the first time I attended a Bible study class. I was appalled that my class members were writing in their Bibles. I mean, they actually took pen to page—underlining words, highlighting phrases, and jotting notes in the margin! Why, I never! I hope I didn't audibly gasp, but I really was unnerved. At some point, Dr. Wright noticed my discomfort and reminded the class that it was perfectly fine to write in their Bibles. While I thought this was sacrilegious, the other members of the class were matter-of-fact about it. The first time I wrote in my Bible, it was a liberating moment. The Bible was less intimidating and more user-friendly. It wasn't long before I was having a conversation with the text—jotting down my questions and responses to what I was reading. Today, I have several Bibles—one of which I don't write in at all; I keep it clean in case I need to photocopy a page. Of course, today, there are all kinds of electronic versions of the Bible, which eliminates the need for a "clean" unmarked text. I continue my old school ways: Bibles for reading and Bibles for studying and marking up! I show my marked-up Bible to every new Bible study class I teach to let them know that it's really okay to write in their Bibles.

The first course in my Bible study curriculum was one I adapted from Trinity UCC, "Bible Basics." This four-week course was the prerequisite for all subsequent courses. We spend the first week getting to know the Bible. I show them my marked-up Bible and encourage them to mark up theirs. Then we look at the table of contents and talk about how the Bible is divided, noting the order of the books, noting how the Bible is organized, looking through the pages, finding specific passages, talking about what makes sense and what is confusing. Over the course of the four weeks, we talk about each section of the Bible and about the major characters and stories. Students begin to perk up because they are familiar with the stories and now have a way of looking at the whole and how familiar stories fit into the larger story of the Bible.

At the end of our time together, we have prayed for God's presence and power, we have shared a bit about who each of us is, and we've explored a book that seemed so untouchable before we started our adventure together. At the end of four weeks, we all have a general sense of the Bible and we all feel more comfortable about asking questions or talking about our fears. With Bible Basics as a foundation, we can move on to other topics.

The benefit of requiring everyone to take a Bible Basics class is that no one feels out of place. Everyone is on the same page, and all have a working knowledge of the Bible. No one will be embarrassed about not knowing where to find Leviticus or James or Jeremiah. You will be better able to determine what sequence of courses to offer based on learners' lingering questions and feedback from the course evaluation. Therefore, your curriculum will need to be flexible early on; as time goes on, you will know what sequence of courses will work well for your congregation.

10

Make Bible Study a Church Event

My Chicago pastor, Rev. Wright, made a point nearly every Sunday to mention believers and church members who did not know the Bible. Every time he waxed on about illiterate Christians, I felt a tinge of guilt. I was one of those folks. I didn't know the Bible and didn't even know why it was important. I resisted the call to Bible study because my knowledge was inadequate and I didn't want to be embarrassed about something I should have known. But week after week, the call grew stronger. I finally mustered up enough courage to attend a class. I was woefully behind. I didn't have the course book yet and the class was already on chapter 10. But the information was so fascinating that I was hooked.

You will want to say something about the importance of Bible study during worship services. Please understand that I am not suggesting that you shame folks into studying the Bible. Instead, lift up the benefits of Bible study when you have the opportunity to do so. Let folks know how enriched their times of worship and their lives will be once they understand the Bible. Worship is a good time to help folks think about how they can deepen their relationship with God, with each other, and with themselves when they explore the riches of the Bible.

A nonthreatening way to get folks excited about Bible study is to host a "Bible Study Fair." Set up a space with various stations; if you have a fellowship hall, this is the perfect venue. Set up tables around the room, each with some aspects related to Bible study. For example, one table could contain various translations of the Bible so students can browse and handle them. Another table can contain Bible study aids: various kinds of commentaries, atlases, concordances, etc. A third table can contain various Bible study books. Students' interest will be piqued when they can actually hold the books, leaf through the pages, and imagine what it would be like to study the book.

Be creative about what kinds of resources are introduced to the congregation. Nothing is off limits. Too often, people harbor the notion that only trained ministers can understand the Bible. What we want to do is empower members to investigate for themselves, share their learnings in community, and remain open to the ways in which we can know the Bible and thereby know God and ourselves.

The point of the fair is to provide the resources that can enhance Bible study in a space conducive to browsing and wandering without the pressure of making a commitment. The materials become less intimidating and much more interesting.

If you already have one or more Bible study classes, ask class members to give short testimonies about how Bible study has helped them in their daily walk of faith. People love to share good news, and what better way to "advertise" Bible study than to have real people talk about the real changes in their lives?

Voice Your Choice: Choosing the Bible That's Right for You

The main text for Bible study is the *Bible*. Did you get that? Surprisingly, I've attended Bible study groups that never referred to the Bible and never used the Bible as the basic text for the class. Encourage people to examine different versions of the Bible for study; you may be surprised at how intimidating the Bible can be. The Bible has topped the bestseller list for decades and there are a multitude of Bibles out there. Choosing one version can be daunting. Help people decide what will work best for them by having the various versions available for them to peruse. One exercise that is helpful is to identify a text and have it read from the various versions to note the differences and nuances of each. Persons may decide to work with more than one version. That's okay.

Here is a quick sample of Bibles that are readily available:

- *The King James Version* (KJV) is the most popular version of the Bible and tends to be the least expensive. King James of England commissioned a version of the Bible that would be authoritative, because there were two English Bibles—the Bishops' Bible and the Geneva Bible. In 1604, a group of theologians and church leaders met to translate the Bible from the original Hebrew and Greek. This version was to be used in all the churches of England. It took the men (yes, the committee was all male) seven years, and in 1611, the KJV was published and widely distributed. The KJV is known for its lyrical renderings: it sounds good when read out loud. But there are problems with the KJV. The translation is based on faulty Greek texts and there are errors in the translation. With the discovery of later texts and a deeper understanding of Hebrew and Greek, there are more reliable sources that are not reflected in the KJV. The style and rhythm of the KJV are familiar but can be intimidating and misleading for some modern readers. While the KJV is good for personal devotions, it is not the best version for critical study unless read alongside versions that reflect newer scholarship. Still, the KJV is the most available version with many editions targeted to specific groups. For example, there is the **African American Jubilee Edition** (New York: American Bible Society, 1999), which bridges the gap between seventeenth-century England and contemporary life for African Americans; it includes supplementary material on African culture, the black church, African American spirituality, music, and worship. **The 400th Anniversary Edition** (Nashville: Thomas Nelson, 2010) includes updated study notes, a concordance, maps, and other supplementary materials. The **KJV Sportsmen's Bible** (Nashville: Broadman and Holman, 2008) includes devotions especially for those who hunt and fish. Promotional materials encourage churches to sponsor wild game dinners as a way to bring people together.

- **The New American Bible** (NAB) was prepared by Catholic scholars and is considered generally accurate in its translation of Hebrew and Greek. The translation is based on Old Greek and Qumran (the Dead Sea Scrolls) texts.
- **The New English Bible** (NEB) is the first British translation to appear after the publication of the KJV. It reflects a bit more contemporary biblical scholarship.
- **The New International Version** (NIV) is the best-selling version of the Bible today. Bookstores (remember those?) often carry more editions of the NIV than others,

including the KJV. The NIV appeared in 1978 and represents a more conservative voice than the Revised Standard Version (RSV). You will find this version in more church pews than any other. The English translations, while more contemporary, reflect more conservative understandings theologically, and the tone is more evangelical. It is the result of work by scholars from England, Australia, Canada, New Zealand, and the United States. This version is targeted and marketed to specific groups (men, women, teens, military personnel) as well as particular themes (stewardship, mission, and ministry).

* *The Jewish Publication Society (JPS) Hebrew-English Tanakh* is the oldest complete Hebrew version of the Bible and includes the JPS English translation. This translation, published in 1985, is based on the Leningrad Codex, which dates back to Aaron Ben Moses ben-Asher (around 930 CE). Ben-Asher's work was revised by Samuel ben Jacob of Egypt in 1010 CE. The manuscript was lost and rediscovered in the mid-nineteenth century. Its format includes two-column pages—one for the Hebrew and the second for the English translation. Explanatory notes and informative articles make the JPS Hebrew-English TANAKH (Philadelphia: JPS, 1985) accessible to most contemporary readers. The translation was done by prominent Jewish biblical scholars and took some thirty years of collaboration.

* *The Bible in Today's English* and *The Good News Bible* (GNB) are not translations, per se. They are actually paraphrases. They do not conform to formal English; they are written in contemporary idioms to appeal to a wide range of readers. Most often, these paraphrases do not try to reconcile difficulties in syntax, images, and idioms that are found when attempting to translate from the Hebrew and Greek.

- *The Revised Standard Version* (RSV) was published in 1952 and was a response to the KJV. The RSV modernized the language but kept the KJV pronouns in referring to God: thee, thy, and thou. For this reason, some scholars objected to its accuracy. However, the RSV employed the use of textual criticism and was an ecumenical venture. The scholars tried to translate the Bible literally from the Hebrew and Greek.

- *The Jerusalem Bible* (JB) is a Roman Catholic translation produced in 1966 during the Second Vatican Council. It uses understandings and learnings from the Dead Sea Scrolls and was translated by biblical scholars of L'École Biblique in Jerusalem. The JB is a fairly accurate French translation of the complete canon of Scripture. From this French original came the English edition, edited by renowned Bible scholar Alexander Jones (London: Darton, Longman & Todd, 1966).

- *The New Revised Standard Version* (NRSV) followed the Revised Standard Version (RSV). The NRSV is fast becoming the most widely used translation. It is the version primarily used in college and seminary classrooms as the standard for critical study of the Bible. It has modernized the King James English and attempts to be inclusive where the Hebrew and Greek intend inclusivity. It tries to avoid masculine pronouns where possible. References to God are still masculine; it does seek to be inclusive and such judgments are considered subjective by some scholars. The translation work included scholars from Protestant, Catholic, Orthodox Christian, and Jewish circles. This Bible is an interfaith and ecumenical product. It generally reflects the latest knowledge of text, Hebrew and Greek grammar, and emerging scholarship. The most popular edition of the NRSV is the *New Oxford Annotated Bible* (New York: Oxford University Press, 1991), a study Bible with ample informative articles. *The Harper Collins Study Bible* (San Francisco, 2006) is produced by the Society of Biblical Literature and is a popular version.

• *The Message* by Eugene H. Peterson (Colorado Springs: NavPress, 2003) is gaining in popularity. Peterson, a pastor and former seminary professor of biblical languages, paraphrases the Bible with a more scholarly and theological base. His aim is to get people to pick up the Bible; he encourages persons to read his version along with a more scholarly version. His language is moving, and this version is attracting a wide range of people.

The point, regardless of choice, is for people to pick up the Bible and begin their study. It is not a bad thing to have multiple versions of the Bible used during Bible study. Let the people choose their version and supplement their choices with additional information and background materials. Just remember that nothing will happen until and unless people are willing to pick up and open the book.

(12)

Use the Right Tools

Okay, so by now, many of you have heard the story of my first forays into carpentry. I was putting up the hardware so I could hang the drapery rod in my living room. When my brother stopped by for a visit, he asked why I was using a butter knife instead of a screwdriver. Yes, yes, yes—I knew better. But I didn't have a screwdriver and didn't want to stop my momentum by going to the hardware store to purchase one. It didn't matter that I was frustrated at how slowly the project was moving or that my hands were already sore and I hadn't gotten one screw into the wall. He went out to his car and returned with two screwdrivers—a slotted and a Phillips. I couldn't believe how easily and quickly the task was accomplished with the right tools! It took the wisdom of my brother to let me know that the right tools can make projects run smoothly and quickly.

I cannot overstate the importance of using the right tools. Whether we are talking about carpentry or Bible study we need to make sure we have the right resources so the task can flow. In Bible study, we find any number of resources—some credible, some so-so, and some just not appropriate.

The tools to enhance Bible study include the following:

* *Bible Commentaries*: these are systematic studies and interpretations of biblical texts. They provide historical background information of the text, explanations of how texts have been interpreted and used throughout the churches, and additional information about various topics related to the text. Commentaries include interpretive work on each book of the Bible; some include work on the Apocrypha, but many do not. Commentaries provide

overviews of the books as well as articles on various topics and aids for teaching and preaching. There are one-volume commentaries but most are multivolume sets. Commentaries are essential tools for Bible study and can cost a pretty penny. A few worthy one-volume commentaries include: *The New Interpreter's Bible One Volume Commentary*, edited by Beverly Roberts Gaventa and David L. Petersen (Nashville: Abingdon Press, 2010); *Eerdmans Commentary on the Bible*, edited by James D. G. Dunn (Grand Rapids: Eerdmans Press, 2003); and, *Harper-Collins Bible Commentary—Revised,* by James L. Mays (New York: HarperOne, 2000). Not all volumes in a set will meet your needs. It is better to take some time examining the volumes before buying a set. Next are some commentaries to consider. *The New Interpreter's Bible* (Nashville: Abingdon Press, 1994–2004) is a twelve-volume set that includes work by a number of scholars and ministers who provide contemporary interpretations of the text for today's student and reflect a diverse understanding of social, racial, and theological contexts. *Interpretation: A Bible Commentary for Teaching and Preaching* (Louisville: Westminster John Knox Press, 2005) is a multivolume set with varying prices for each book that is geared specifically to those who preach and teach. It seeks to relate the texts to real, everyday life. *Hermeneia* is a commentary series (Minneapolis: Fortress Press) that takes a serious and critical look at the texts based on the original Hebrew and Greek as well as other related sources. *The Daily Bible Study* series by William Barclay (Scottish theologian and professor) is an affordable, seventeen-volume set and is accessible to the average reader. Scholars have major concerns about Barclay's work, but his scholarship is solid, though dated in some areas. He is a good read and can be a good place to start with igniting your congregation through Bible study.

◆ *Bible Atlases:* a book of maps will tell a lot about the lands being studied. An atlas is more than just about geography; a good one will provide information about climate, people, animal and plant life, and topography. An atlas will show the location of cities and towns, the physical characteristics of the land, national and territorial borders, as well as trade, commercial, military, and travel routes. In addition, an atlas will help people connect sites with each other—folk will have some sense of the distance between places, what barriers prevent free flow travel, and how sites relate to each other. Some are surprised, for instance, to learn that so much of the action of the Bible happens in Africa. Many don't realize that Egypt is part of the African continent. They will have a sense of being there when identifying Sinai, the Dead Sea, Hebron, Bethlehem, Galilee—geography becomes the backdrop for the action of the Bible. One gets to picture the various hills, valleys, rivers, deserts, and lush oases that make up biblical lands. An atlas is important for those who have not traveled to the Holy Land. It's not the same as being there, but an atlas can help. Scholars debate the historicity of various sites as they seek to connect ancient places with contemporary knowledge—the search for accuracy continues. But a good atlas will help us envision what the Bible tells us. A few good atlases: the *Oxford Bible Atlas* (New York: Oxford University Press, 2007) includes recent advances in biblical, archaeological, and topographical scholarship; *The HarperCollins Concise Atlas of the Bible* (New York: HarperOne, 1997) includes a chronology of events and an index of names, places, biblical references, over 250 maps, and site archaeological reconstructions; *The Zondervan NIV Atlas of the Bible* (Grand Rapids: Regency Reference

Library, 1989) has more than 200 photographs, illustrations, maps, and charts as well as a glossary and scripture index.

● **Bible Dictionaries:** these work just like other dictionaries and are keyed to the Bible. Look up a word, name, place, or theological concept, and you will find short articles providing useful information. Bible dictionaries, like commentaries, may be of one or multivolume. There are several good and affordable ones on the market: *The New Interpreter's Dictionary of the Bible* is a four-volume set (Nashville: Abingdon Press, 2006) compiled by a diverse group of women and men reflecting a wide range of religious, geographical, theological, racial, and cultural backgrounds; the *HarperCollins Bible Dictionary* (San Francisco: HarperSanFrancisco, 1996) is a single volume that includes informative articles on the Dead Sea Scrolls and a number of maps that highlight the politics and territorial boundaries of biblical times; also one volume, the *Eerdmans Dictionary of the Bible* (Grand Rapids, Mich.: Eerdmans, 2000) is illustrated and provides a range of theological perspectives.

● **Bible Concordances:** a concordance is an alphabetical list of every word in the Bible that tells you where that word can be found in the Bible. Some concordances include Hebrew and Greek lexicons providing the transliteration of the original language and background information about the word itself. This tool is essential when you can only remember a word or phrase of a passage. Some concordances are exhaustive (listing every word in the Bible) while others list major words. The thing to be sure about with concordances is to make sure it is keyed to the version of the Bible you are using—otherwise you will become frustrated looking for a word that is not used in that version. The most popular concordance is *Strong's*

Exhaustive Concordance of the Bible (Nashville: Abingdon, 1986) and it is keyed to the King James Version; therefore, you may be hard pressed to find the words used in the New Revised Standard Version. *The New International Bible Concordance* (Grand Rapids: Zondervan, 1998) accompanies the New International Version, and the *Concise Concordance to the New Revised Standard Version* (New York: Oxford University Press, 1993) accompanies the NRSV.

Students may try out various tools before they find the ones that work for them. Assure them that it's okay and the important thing is to find tools with which they are most comfortable.

13

Tie Bible Study to Worship

Christian churches are communities of word and sacrament. We gather as God's people to confess our sins, to forgive one another and ourselves, to pray for others and for creation, to extend hospitality and love, to be fortified for works towards peace and justice, to hear God's Word, and to celebrate God's presence in our midst. In addition, we witness to and celebrate the baptism of those who accept God's invitation into God's household. We commemorate Christ's sacrifice at the communion table. Through our prayers, worship, and sacraments, we rehearse God's gracious acts and celebrate God's love, grace, and mercy towards us.

A way to ignite your congregation is to use the lectionary for preaching *and* Bible study. A lectionary is a weekly schedule of biblical passages to be read and heard in the worldwide gathered communities of Christians. A lectionary will list biblical books, selected chapters, and particular verses for reading and studying. Some lectionaries include information or suggestions for using the designated texts. Lectionary-based congregations will all hear and explore the same scripture on any given Sunday, regardless of denomination or geographical location. Christians all over the world focus on the same texts.

The aim of a lectionary is to provide a way to read major sections of the Bible in an orderly fashion. The most widely used lectionary is the Revised Common Lectionary (RCL) used by Catholics and Protestants. The schedule of readings includes a passage from the Hebrew Bible, the Apocrypha (for Catholic circles) or the Acts of the Apostles; a passage from one of the psalms; another from either Revelation or the epistles; and a passage from one of the four Gospels. The schedule of readings is a three-year cycle, with each year focusing on one of the Synoptic Gospels:

- Year A: Matthew beginning with the first Sunday of Advent in 2013, 2016, 2019, etc.
- Year B: Mark beginning with the first Sunday of Advent in 2014, 2017, etc.
- Year C: Luke beginning with the first Sunday of Advent in 2012, 2015, 2018, etc.

The Gospel of John does not have a designated year, but parts of it are used at various points in the church season—Christmas, Lent, and Easter. The lectionary takes persons on a journey through the church year, beginning with the first Sunday of Advent, and moves through Christmas, Epiphany, Ash Wednesday, Lent, Palm Sunday, Maundy Thursday, Good Friday, Easter, Ascension Sunday, Pentecost, and "ordinary time," following Pentecost. The cycle then begins again. The lectionary is a tool to shape worship, which makes it conducive to a parallel Bible study. The lectionary allows preacher and people to read and study the same passages and ensures that members will have a comprehensive understanding of the Bible and the church year.

By preaching from the same text that is used in Bible study, you allow people the opportunity to explore, meditate upon, and reflect on the text more fully before Sunday. After living with the texts for a week, members will bring a deeper understanding of the text to Sunday worship. They will see a bigger picture of how all the parts of worship—call to worship, prayers, music, mission—fit together. This is an excellent way to engage members of the congregation in studying and worship and to ignite the congregation.

14

Create Gender Specific Courses

Once people have established the habit of attending Bible study, build on that. My new home church, Mt. Zion Congregational UCC in Cleveland, hosts a Bible study for the women of the church. Sisters in the Spirit meet the first Friday of every month. At the December session, the group convenes at an area restaurant to study and share a meal. At that meeting, donations are collected for that year's charity—usually a shelter that provides services to women and their children in various stages of transition. Each book chosen for study is a woman-focused Bible study. The group is intergenerational and includes single, married, divorced, and widowed women. The books chosen are recommended by members of the group. Each session starts with a short check-in, a prayer, and a summary of the previous week's learnings. The conversation is always lively and animated; the group is hard pressed to honor the time boundaries. At the end of the session, there is a benediction and snacks. The women spend some time after the session chatting and checking in with each other.

A pastor in Connecticut has been intentional about periodically highlighting the learnings of the women's Bible study in worship. She uses woman-focused materials for the women's weekly Bible study. At the end of each course, she and the members of the class share their learnings in worship. When I happened to visit one Sunday, I was shocked to see all the women in their sleeping clothes—some wore pajamas, most had on house slippers, some wore hair rollers and chenille bathrobes—they had just finished studying a book and they thought a "pajama party" was the perfect way to share their learnings. The men were amused and a tad jealous. They, too, wanted a fun Bible study. The pastor trained one of the elders in the church and helped the men select a male-focused Bible study resource. The men could hardly wait to stage their own time of sharing with the rest of the congregation. Needless to say, at each of these special worship services, everyone was interested to hear what the women and men had to say. This was a fun way to keep the importance of Bible study before the congregation.

Don't leave the men out! My home church also sponsors a Bible study specifically for the men, Men of the Word. In a relaxed setting, men gather once monthly to study the Bible and to share aspects of their lives. In a noncompetitive atmosphere, men have the opportunity to support each other around the various areas of concerns they identify: family concerns, parenting, life-work balance, health and wellness, grief and sorrow, finances, friendships, and sports.

Men who participate in the Bible study state that they feel a sense of belonging and are building trust and friendships with the other men in the church. They plan several activities throughout the year, including a day of golfing. In addition, as a bona fide entity within the church, they host coffee hours and raise funds, which they donate to the operating budget of the church. There is a growing list of Bible studies targeted specifically for men:

- *The Daily Bible Study for Men* by Stuart Briscoe (Carol Stream, Ill.: Tyndale House Publishers, 1999) is a topical Bible study for men;
- *The Men of Color Study Bible* (Nashville: World Bible Publishing, 2002) is based on the KJV and is targeted to men of African descent with reference materials written by, for, and about men of color to strengthen their faith and empower their witness;

- ***Quiet Strength: Men's Study Bible*** by Tony Dungy and Karl Leuthauser (Loveland, Colo.: Group Publishing, 2007) is composed of six Bible studies, crafted especially for men to provide biblical answers, relationship-building discussion questions, fun activities, and character-building insights from the life of Super Bowl XLI Winning Head Coach Tony Dungy.
- ***The New Men's Devotional Bible*** by Thomas Smith (Grand Rapids: Zondervan Publishing, 2006) is available in print and electronic forms. It is based on the NIV.

While there is something to be said about gathering as one body, do not underestimate the power of gender-specific Bible study groups to ignite your congregation. Both groups agree that there are things that can be effectively explored in same-gender groups. In both instances, it is important to set some guidelines to engender trust and camaraderie.

⑮

Involve the Whole Person

Bible study is most fun when it appeals to all the senses. When I was training to be a teacher, we understood that students learned in different ways. No particular way was better than the others; the methods were different. If we wanted to be effective teachers, we needed to use all of the methods at some point in our teaching. So I devised lessons that appealed to sight, sound, taste, touch, and smell. Both children and adults profit when learning embraces as many of the senses as possible.

My Christian Education professor in seminary, Dr. Dorothy Jean Furnish, taught us that people discover meaning when they "experience" the Bible. This is true no matter what age group your Bible study class falls into. What does it mean to experience the Bible? One thing it means is helping people place themselves into the text as if they were part of the intended, original audience.

My own praxis embraces the concept of experiencing the Bible for all learners, from the youngest to the most mature. We all gain something when we can use our imaginations while reading and studying the Bible. What works for children can work for adults—adults, too, want to feel something when they study the Bible. The ways to help people enter the stories of the Bible is more complex than the right brain–left brain dichotomy. Faith is deepened when we can explore the Bible more fully and using both sides of the brain.

One way of experiencing the Bible is by using Howard Gardner's "multiple intelligences." The following is adapted from Barbara Bruce's *7 Ways of Teaching the Bible to Adults: Using*

Our Multiple Intelligences to Build Faith (Nashville: Abingdon Press, 2000). Based on Gardner's work, Bruce provides a blueprint for implementing the seven modes for Bible study. Gardner contends that people learn in at least seven ways:

- Verbal and linguistic: this mode calls on the skills of reading, writing, speaking, and listening; it is the most common mode used for Bible study since we use these skills in everyday life and interactions;
- Logical and mathematical: this mode is based in logic, is linear, and focuses on problem-solving; the important skill is reason and is implemented through exploring cause-and-effect, solving puzzles, and establishing timelines;
- Visual and spatial: this mode is based on what is seen; implementation includes using props, pictures, and film clips, as well as visualization exercises, mind-mapping, and guided imagery;
- Bodily and kinesthetic: this mode requires physical movement and is implemented through any kind of movement, the handling of objects, body prayer, role-playing, and breathing techniques;
- Musical and rhythmic: this mode relies on sounds and will include singing, dancing, playing musical instruments, humming, clapping hands, and tapping feet;
- Interpersonal: this mode requires interacting with others; implementation includes group projects, one-to-one conversations, and communal activities;
- Intrapersonal: this mode is about "me time;" persons are introspective and reflective; implementation includes journaling, silent meditation, writing letters.

No one activity will touch on all the intelligences. And the intelligences are not discrete modes; they will overlap and intermingle.

The point is to mix up your class methodology to include these various modes in order to reach the largest number of students. Some adults will be shy about some of them, but if you create an atmosphere of trust, students will risk being vulnerable and silly in order to learn and have fun.

To ignite your congregation through Bible study, you want to have as much variety as possible to create and maintain lively and engaging Bible studies.

16

Set a Time Limit for Teachers

As a pastor, I had a difficult time getting folks to volunteer for various positions in the church. The most frequent excuse given was the person didn't have the time. I suggested a trial or probation period, just to see if the person and position were a match. I asked people to consider serving for three weeks and we would do an assessment.

As it is with most church positions, people don't want the responsibility of leading a class because they might get "stuck" doing it forever. A probationary period allows the person the opportunity to test drive the job and see if it works for them. It was the rare case where the person opted out after the probation period. Then, once the person said yes, we signed a covenant stating the length of service, expectations for getting the job done, and promises for support, training, evaluation, and whatever else the person felt was needed for success. Expectations might include a break if the class lasted more than four or five weeks. The break might be for students and instructor or just for the instructor. Let the instructor help develop the covenant. Members were happy knowing there were parameters, expectations, and support.

At the end of their term of service, they were offered the opportunity to sign up again or move on to another opportunity. Regardless of their decision, they were recognized in a worship service designed to show appreciation for their service and to pray for them as they continued their service or moved on to something else. Always make sure to thank folks who serve!

Develop Bible Study Rituals

It is important to have a ritual for your Bible study. Rituals are things done repeatedly and collectively to establish, reinforce, and support group identity. Furthermore, rituals form and support social and spiritual bonds among class members. The ritual marks the Bible study as a sacred time and serves as a benediction at the end of the session.

The ritual you develop can be simple: open and close with prayer. Some other ritual activities to consider include:

- A check-in time: sharing what's happened since the last class session; these can be brief updates;
- A time of testimony: sharing how God has blessed members since the last class, especially if a member has asked for prayers about a particular concern;
- Lighting candles and a time for quiet reflection: I found this especially helpful for classes that convened after working hours. It provided a time for students to take a deep breath and settle down after a time of getting to the church through traffic or on public transportation;
- Sharing a light supper: soup and salad or snacks. This is helpful for folks who come to Bible study right after work and don't have time for dinner before the class; they appreciate having something light to stave off hunger pangs;
- Breath work: an intentional time of inhaling and exhaling; this helps people to center and focus on the upcoming study;
- Playing music as students enter the class or study space: the music can be lively or meditative; or you can mix the music up—one class meditative, the next more upbeat;

- A time to observe any additions to the space: posters, photographs, papers, art work;
- A time to extend blessings to each other: the wording can be fairly straightforward, "My hope for us during this Bible study is that we come to understand forgiveness more fully. "
- A review of the previous lesson: what was covered, any observations made, questions raised and lingering; the review can happen at the beginning of the session or at the close;
- Closing prayer with members standing and holding hands: the teacher can pray, members can rotate the time of prayer, or a group prayer can be done.

The ritual should be a way to open and a way to close each Bible study session. Ask students for suggestions.

18

Sneak in Mini–Bible Studies

Before I started an official Bible study class at the church I served in Chicago, I started giving mini–Bible studies. I began all church and committee meetings with a short devotional. The devotional included singing, prayer, scripture, and Bible study. The scripture was selected based on the business at hand. The aim of the Bible study was to illuminate and inform the work of the committee or meeting. Persons were thrilled to learn that the Bible had so much to say about congregational life. They began to look forward to these devotionals. It was later that I shared my ulterior motive: getting them excited about the Bible by opening it and seeing what's really there.

By the time I announced the first Bible study class, they were primed and ready to study. This may sound a little sneaky, but the purpose is right on target. The mini–Bible studies set the tone for the work to be carried out and helped folks to center and focus. The Bible studies also served to remind us all about why we were engaged in the work of the church. Sneaky? Maybe. Does it work? Absolutely!

19

Train New Bible Study Teachers

Always have folks in the wings ready to assume teaching responsibilities. Encourage your more enthusiastic and competent students to consider teaching. Provide the support they may need or want, such as time to think about the courses with a small group. What resources will they need? What specialized knowledge would be helpful? Let their questions and concerns guide the kind of training you provide.

When I was a pastor in Chicago, I knew I could only only so many Bible study classes. My students were eager but didn't feel confident to take on teaching adults. I selected three of my best students and asked if they would be willing to team teach. They were hesitant but I assured them that I would provide all the training they needed. They agreed and the fun began.

By this time in our life together, I had taught Bible Basics as well as Saved, Sanctified, and Filled with the Holy Spirit: Selected Christian Doctrines. The classes consisted of church members and persons from the neighborhood who were invited to the classes. As new persons joined, they needed to take Bible Basics. The three students I selected and trained agreed to team teach Bible Basics. They were terrific teachers; they added things to the class that I didn't think about because their experience was still fresh.

When I added another class, Exploring the Gospels, I wanted one of the three to teach Saved, Sanctified, and Filled with the Holy Spirit. One student, in particular, volunteered to teach the class solo. I attended the first session or two to observe his teaching. We spent some time after class to debrief his experience and to see if there were lingering questions or concerns. I was very proud of my students who became teachers. We celebrated their gifts during worship services and the entire congregation affirmed them. And the teaching staff grew from there. Members volunteered to teach classes they had completed. By the time I left the church, there were six active Bible study classes, and I only taught one.

Students in the classes were encouraged; some wanted to teach but needed some help. They knew that they, too, could break open God's Word for the rest of the members. The Bible study teachers also became active worship leaders. They were much more confident and sure of themselves.

Don't be afraid to encourage persons to become teachers. Assure them that they will be trained and supported. This calling out of gifts will ignite your congregation and encourage others to participate in Bible study.

(20)

Be Prepared

Bible study requires time and effort. Do not wait until the last minute to think about what you will teach. This is where a course syllabus will be helpful. Make a plan, gather your resources, and think about the flow of the class. Bathe your planning with prayer and reflection. You may want to engage a group of conversation partners to help you think through what you want to teach and how you will teach.

Even after you have done the preliminary planning, spend some time prior to each session in prayer. Review what happened at the last session; reflect on the questions your students asked; anticipate questions related to the upcoming session. Make any necessary adjustments before the class gathers.

Make sure you have all the resources you need, that you know how to work any equipment you will be using, that you have ample copies of any handouts. A few minutes thinking about your class will pay dividends for your students and for you. It pays to be prepared.

21

Pass the Handouts

This may seem like an unnecessary task but it will pay off in the long run. Students like to know what's planned and how the class will proceed. Begin each course with a tentative syllabus. A syllabus is an overview of the course and includes the course title, instructor, any contact information, meeting times and places, expectations, various policies (attendance, grading, expected behaviors, conversation guidelines, etc.), order of topics to be covered, any project or exam dates and deadlines, required readings and related questions or activities. The syllabus does not have to be lengthy but should provide students with information about what the course is about, the purpose for the course, how the course will be taught, and what is required to complete the course successfully.

The syllabus is a guide, not a document written in stone. I always place a statement in the syllabus that the stated agenda is subject to change based on the movement of the Holy Spirit. My experience with Bible study is that there needs to be flexibility—some discussions and activities will take longer than planned. You want to provide a space for meaningful learning and sometimes that means suspending the syllabus.

In addition to the syllabus, you will want to have handouts throughout the course. You don't have to have one for each session, but it will be helpful to students to have periodic outlines, overview, additional information—whatever you think will enhance the learning experience.

Handouts provide many opportunities for class members to work with materials after the class and in between class sessions. If your congregation has made a commitment to being green, encourage students to bring their laptops or tablet notebooks to take notes to cut down on the use of paper. You can e-mail handouts to students who can print them out as needed.

22

Evaluate, Evaluate, Evaluate

It is important to gauge how things are going with your Bible studies—both the overall program and individual courses. Evaluation provides feedback and should not be seen as an indictment on the program or its instructors. Develop an attitude that evaluation is good.

The evaluation process does not have to be elaborate. Congratulate students for completing the course. For more candid answers, do not require them to identify themselves or to sign the form. Ask the following questions:

- What did you find most helpful about the course? Why was this helpful for you?
- What did you find least helpful? What can be done to improve this?
- What was missing that you wanted to explore in the course?
- What can the instructor do to improve his or her teaching?
- Would you recommend this course to your friends? Why or why not?
- What additional information and feedback do you want the instructor to know?

In other words, an evaluation is seeking feedback on what the students learned, why what they learned is important, what worked and what didn't, and suggestions to improve the course and teaching.

Do not be intimidated by or afraid of evaluations. They are tools to help your planning. Evaluation is your friend!

23

Celebrate!

Always make time to celebrate—the curriculum, your instructors, and your students. My home church in Chicago, Trinity United Church of Christ, set the tone for celebration. At the end of each semester, there was a time set aside in the worship service to acknowledge the teachers and students engaged in Bible study. The names of the students were called (just like at graduation), and they were presented with certificates of completion. The pastor prayed for them and their instructors. At the end of worship, the congregation gathered in the fellowship hall for a reception honoring those who had completed Bible study courses.

Students were selected to share how Bible study changed their faith walk and their lives. These testimonies were moving and affirmed the value of group study. Do not underestimate the power of celebration in igniting your church.

A church-wide celebration is a fitting close to the end of a Bible study cycle. Other members of the congregation were encouraged to seek out Bible study classes. And a new season of Bible study was ready to be launched.

Celebrate! Celebrate! Celebrate!

Part II

THE GOOD STUFF:
METHODS AND STRATEGIES

Once you have started Bible study classes, you will want to keep them energized and interesting. What follows are ways, methods, and strategies for the actual Bible studies. The suggestions are not exhaustive; they are designed to fire your imaginations. Be bold and experiment with various other methods and strategies. Remember that the purpose of incorporating Bible study is to ignite your congregation to open the book of our faith. Bible study can be informative, life-changing, and fun.

24

Book It!

A way of getting into Bible study is to read and study it book by book. There are a number of resources to help in this endeavor. There are programs that enable one to read the entire Bible in a year. This ambitious plan works for many. A concern is the depth of study that can happen when the goal is to get through the Bible within a set time. Here, a thoughtful curriculum is important.

The easiest way to get folks engaged is to start with the Gospels. The Gospels are a lot less intimidating than most of the books of the Hebrew Bible. And the Gospels likely will be more familiar. You can assign readings for each week and provide some starter questions: Who wrote this book? Who is the intended audience? Who are the major players in the text? What is the conflict or point of tension? What are the outcomes in the text? How do the texts relate to church life or life outside the church?

After the Gospels, you may want to continue in the New Testament or move to the Hebrew Bible. Since the Gospels are based on promises, characters, and actions in the Hebrew Bible, it would not be out of line to move to it after a study of the Gospels.

Or you may want to start with the Psalms. The poetry, prayers, and songs lend themselves to deeply moving exploration. You will want to provide some basic information about the psalms: the likely author, the situation that give rise to the particular psalm, the need being lifted up. The Psalms allow persons to connect the circumstances of the Bible with the real, everyday lives of the class members. Some will have fond memories of some verses that have provided comfort over the years. Some will be puzzled by the depth of emotions found in the Psalms. Most will be able to relate in some form or fashion to the Psalms.

If you decide to explore the Psalms, you may want to introduce the discipline of journaling, if your members are not already familiar with it. This is an opportunity for people to write down their thoughts, feelings, and questions safely. Persons are invited to share as they are willing. They will learn that they share much with the writers of the Psalms: feelings of being abandoned or used, anger, fear, anxiety, joy, relief, support, and affirmation. All of these emotions and more are expressed in the Psalms.

However you decide to proceed, know that book-by-book is a systematic way to approach the Bible. As persons move through the Bible, they will gain greater confidence and will want to continue the journey towards becoming more biblically literate.

25

Get Theological

Many church members are struggling to make sense of life and the challenges it presents. A Bible study that deals with the big questions of life can be transformative. Something marvelous can happen when a group of people gather to ponder the important questions of life: Who am I? Where did I come from? What is my purpose in life? What contribution am I called to make? What happens when I die? Why do the good die young? Why do fools fall in love?

Any and all of these questions and more are the basis for lively Bible study. While the Bible may not answer every question, there will be ample material to help people think through their questions. This will provide the opportunity to see that the Bible is not a ready-answer book but rather provides guidelines for decision-making based on a deep relationship with the God who loves and judges.

When I was a pastor, I was excited about all the things I learned in seminary. I felt that if I could help my members think theologically, they would be empowered to take greater risks for the sake of the gospel. As mentioned above I created a Bible study class entitled "Saved, Sanctified, and Filled with the Holy Spirit: Selected Christian Doctrines." The purpose of the seven-week class was to provide a forum for members to explore some concepts that they had questions about. Topics included faith and doubt, sin and evil, judgment, grace, repentance and salvation, and eschatology. Pretty heavy topics, but I used film clips, music, and art to help the class get handles on the concepts.

At the end of the class, students made presentations along the lines of "how my mind has changed." Students were thoroughly engaged in the Bible study and requested a Part 2. The second class explored the virgin birth, incarnation, atonement, baptism, communion, worship, and hymnology. As part of the second class, I invited guest speakers from various arenas (mental health practitioners, promoters of health and wellness, funeral home directors, a Catholic priest, hospice nurse, and other pastors) to share their understandings and perspectives. Each class session was lively and people felt empowered to voice their own opinions and discomfort with biblical texts and how the church has developed them.

By exploring current events or concerns of the church, you can frame your Bible study so that people are excited. We live in a time of rapid change, and chronic anxiety is the norm. People are worried about their families, their work, and their future. The news stories about impending catastrophes and disasters keep us on edge and fearful about what will happen next. Solid Bible study can help people realize that there is nothing new under the sun. And while the Bible doesn't address all of our ills, it does speak a word of peace, hope, endurance, and love during anxious times. What better way to ignite your congregation than through the stories of God's people who weather the storms of life and fortune and maintain hope in the midst of rapid change.

26

Who Is That?
Character and Personality

People like to star gaze and gossip. By stars, I'm not talking about celestial wonders. Rather, I'm referring to those whom we lift up as celebrities. And there is no shortage of stars in the Bible. Of course, when we explore their stories, they seem like anything but stars. Moses, the great liberator, has a speech impediment—not the picture of the dashing leading man. Further, he tries to get out of an assignment from God. He comes up with all manner of excuses, for which God has an answer. Add to that his anger management problem and Moses is not your likely candidate for stardom. There is something so familiar about Moses that we feel as if we know him.

When we meet Esther, she appears as just another pretty face. She is tutored by the eunuchs on the latest fashion and make-up tips. She auditions to be the next queen. (Her story would make a great reality show.) She is reluctant to take on any leadership tasks; she just wants to live in the lap of luxury that being queen will afford her. She musters the courage to do the unthinkable. She is shrewd and has perfect timing. In stepping up to the plate, she saves her people—an unlikely heroine. Somehow we can relate to her desire to just live quietly and avoid the demands of her people. Yet we applaud her savvy and courage.

And so it is with so many of the persons we encounter in the Bible. The Bible is not a dead, dry book (although parts of it will challenge this assertion). It is filled with interesting men and women who show us what faithfulness and infidelity look like. They deliver poignant lines and give lofty speeches. At the same time, they make foolish choices and state the obvious. They know exactly what they are doing, and they have no clue. Some get it, and we are relieved. Some never do, and we rant and rail against them.

Bible study can be a simple exploration of character and personality. We can try to get behind who the person is, what is motivating him, how she reaches conclusions—and it's just a small step to put ourselves in the biblical story. What would we do? How can we be sure that we would make better choices and decisions? Such questions make for powerful study and reflection. And this can lead to greater commitment to mission and ministry as we try to do better than our biblical ancestors. By putting the biblical characters under a microscope, we bring them to life and allow them to speak to us across the ages. If we can connect with them, surely we can connect with God.

A way to start is to ask members to name as many biblical characters as they can. As they call out names, they will remember other people in the Bible. Members of the class will help each other remember. You may want to ask for a short description of the biblical character named: Jonah was swallowed by a whale, Eve ate an apple off the tree. Let this be a time of sharing; you can fill in the blanks and correct inaccuracies during the course of the study. This approach honors what folks know (or think they know) about the Bible already and gives them the opportunity to shape what they will be studying. It also gives you some sense of where you will need to go with the class to make the experience rich and full.

Delve into the biblical character's personality using contemporary understandings of human nature, family of origin issues, family systems, and mental health and disorders. This can be a fun exercise: by looking at our biblical ancestors, we are also looking at ourselves.

Talk, Talk, Talk

Lecture and discussion are two ways to do Bible study. These methods are most familiar because they don't require much. And they are effective for many. A simple way to get folks into the text is to have a few people read the passage in its entirety. If the class is small, each person can take a verse or two. After the passage is read out loud, ask the following questions:

- Who "wrote" this book or passage?
- What does the text say? Sometimes people think they know the text and are surprised when they read it. For instance, we all are familiar with the scene in the Garden of Eden when Eve gives Adam the apple. The text does not name an apple as the fruit nor does Eve manipulate Adam into eating. She offers the fruit and he takes it.
- Who was the intended audience for this text?
- What did this text mean to the original audience?
- What do we need to know in order to understand the text's context? That is, what historical, political, social, theological, and cultural factors shape the text as we have it?
- How has the meaning of the text changed over time and circumstances from biblical days to today?
- What does the text mean for us today? What contemporary factors (historical, social, political, theological, and cultural) shape how we understand the text?

These questions will lead to more questions and generate good conversation about the text. This method requires some preparation, but the point is to get people talking about the text.

Another method to consider is one called the "African Bible Study" method. The Bible study begins with prayer and proceeds as follows:

- One person reads the text slowly;
- Each person notes a word or phrase that stands out to him or her;
- Without going into lengthy explanations, each person shares the word or phrase that stood out;
- Another person reads the same text slowly; it is helpful if the second reading is from a different translation;
- Each person notes how the text relates to his or her everyday life;
- Each shares how the text relates to his or her life;
- A third person reads the text slowly (from a different translation, if possible);
- Each person reflects on the questions: Given this text, what is God calling me to be or do? Is God inviting me to change in any way?
- Each person shares his or her answers;
- The group discusses what they heard both from the text and other members of the class.
- Close the class session with prayer.

The method can be modified to work for your group. This method is easy to engage because it doesn't require a lot of preparation time. You can provide background information on the text, but I recommend you wait until the class has gone through the process. The background information may change the way people see and understand the text. This method invites persons into community, to share part of their personal story, and provides a communal perspective on the text. It is always interesting to see how people read and understand the text in their own context and situation. The conversation should be enlightening and lively.

28

Set the Stage

Just as we prepare the sanctuary for worship, we should give thought to how to prepare a space for Bible study. If we consider any space in a church building to be sacred ground, we want to show evidence in the space itself. Many adult Bible study groups meet in Sunday school rooms prepared for children. Notice that there are bulletin boards, colorful drawings, many done by the children themselves. There may be learning stations and materials for arts and crafts. Mostly, the adults will ignore these resources since they are "for the children."

I feel, though, that we should prepare a space for adult learners, too. Adults are captured by colorful art work and music. I continue to be surprised by adults who want time to look at things related to Bible study and the space itself.

I love using props in my Bible study classes. I keep a box of props that I take with me when I am leading a Bible study class. If, for instance, the study focuses on Jezebel, I will use a small table that I cover with a colorful cloth (a tablecloth works, too). On top of it, I will place tea light candles that I light (with permission). These I place at the back of the table so those who wish to examine the other items more closely will not burn themselves. I place several mirrors on the table, along with hair brushes and various items of makeup—eye shadow, blushes, lipstick, mascara, eyeliner pencils and different sizes of makeup brushes. I also add pieces of jewelry, many of which previous classes have donated to the prop box. I also place small bottles of perfume and cologne around the mirrors. I once stayed at a hotel in San Francisco called Diva (seriously, I'm not making this up!). I kept the stationery provided in the room—several sheets of letterhead, several envelopes, and a couple of postcards. Each piece has the word "Diva" written on it in prominent letters. Next to the stationery, I place a book embosser that resembles a press that is used to seal letters with a bit of wax. When possible, I also place a small platter of fruits and vegetables that become snacks for the class during the Bible study.

As the students enter the room, they are curious about the table of props, and I allow some time for them to explore the goodies on the table. After greeting the class, having a short check-in, and leading an opening prayer, I ask them to tell me what they know about Jezebel. Inevitably, they usually jump right in about her being a harlot, loose woman, a tease. I acknowledge their comments and then we read several texts related to Jezebel (1 Kings 16, 18, 21). The props illustrate the story and myths surrounding Jezebel. These make the class more interesting and intriguing, especially when we explore the texts and discover that there is nothing sensual about her or her actions.

You can set the stage for almost any story in the Bible. It only takes a bit of time and some imagination. You can even assign small groups to prepare the space for the next Bible study session. It is amazing how creative students can be when given permission and the space to let their imaginations soar.

29

Use the Arts

Throughout the ages, sacred art has been created to illustrate biblical events, characters, and concepts. Catholicism generated a mass of artistic expressions that go back to ancient days, including stained-glass windows, statues, and paintings. The Protestant Reformation, on the other hand, focused on establishing a literary tradition based on biblical texts, including poetry, diaries, orations, sermons, prayers, and various other forms of prose.

As we have seen over recent years, schools that need to cut back programs usually start with the arts and physical education. The church can seize this opportunity to reclaim the fine arts, for they serve to embody the history and values of a people. And the arts represent a legacy for future generations about how we see ourselves in relation to creation and to each other.

The Bible is filled with references to art and music. In fact, the Psalms are songs and litanies often used in worship during biblical times. We should take every opportunity to incorporate the arts into Bible study.

Visual Arts

A great deal of Western art has been shaped and influenced by biblical themes and characters. Reproductions of religious paintings and sculpture are readily available. Or you can plan a visit to your local art museum and ask for a guided tour. You will be amazed at the variety of art displayed and how it relates to the Bible. Don't limit your use of visual arts to paintings and sculpture. Take a look around your church. If yours has stained-glass windows or icons, have someone who is knowledgable take your class on a tour and explain why pieces were chosen and what they represent. Or visit a church that has interesting architecture and décor. For instance, several churches in the San Francisco Bay Area are known for their stained-glass windows: Allen Temple Baptist Church in Oakland, St. Gregory of Nyssa Episcopal Church in San Francisco, and Northbrae Community Church in Berkeley come to mind. Check out the churches in your area and plan a trip. It can be enlightening and will strengthen your Bible study.

Music

No one can dispute the power of music. Music is universal and should be used often. You can have music playing as students enter the room; use music as part of the opening and closing rituals for the class. Use various kinds of sacred music and don't overlook the contribution to this genre by jazz musicians and composers such as Duke Ellington, Louie Bellson, Mary Lou Williams, Seattle Women's Jazz Orchestra, Margaret Bonds, Lesa Terry, and Kimberly Diaz. Others to consider: Sweet Honey in the Rock, John Coltrane, the Sounds of Blackness. There is a branch of hip hop performers that engages religious values and themes: Common, Mos Def, Kanye West, Dead Prez, Talib Kweli, Zion I, and Gift of Gab. Gospel music, including both Negro spirituals and contemporary Gospel music, is a wonderful source to illustrate and support your Bible studies. Be sure to include music from a variety of racial and ethnic groups as well as international pieces. You can borrow CDs from the public library or ask students to bring in music that they find beautiful and spiritual. A search on *www.youtube.com* will provide short videos of various performances. Don't be afraid to branch out and discover new forms of sacred music. Of course, you have a collection of hymns, praise songs, and choruses in your church's hymnal. Pull them out and get the group singing. You will never regret it! I always got good responses by asking students to sing in class. I was nervous at first because I'm not a singer. But students appreciated the attempts and usually someone more skilled would take over in leading the singing. The point is that we gathered to make a joyful noise to God and the songs illuminated some aspect of the Bible study. And it was a nice icebreaker and a way to center folks for the study at hand.

Dramatic Arts

The use of film can be quite effective as a Bible study tool. There are a multitude of films with explicit religious and biblical themes. Most in the following list are readily available on DVD and can be checked out of your local public library. This list is not exhaustive but serves to illustrate the possibilities. Consider viewing parts of the following: *The Ten Commandments, Ben-Hur, The Passion of Christ, Jesus Christ Superstar!, Body and Soul, Elmer Gantry, Romero, The Last Temptation of Christ, The Mission, Lilies of the Field, Raiders of the Lost Ark,* and *Song of Bernadette,* among others. Consider, also, more popular culture films, such as *The Matrix, Woman Thou Art Loosed, Sister Act, The Day After, Mama I Want to Sing, Malcolm X, Osama, Dogma, Bruce Almighty, Saved!, Doubt, Stigmata, Leap of Faith, The Apostle, Gandhi, The Exorcist, There Will Be Blood, Groundhog Day,* and *The Joy Luck Club* as well as television shows like *Amen, Big Love,* and *West Wing.* Be on the lookout for films and cable and television shows that can be used in Bible study. This methodology makes use of television shows, DVDs, or Blu-Ray discs. You can make use of broadcast programming to enhance your Bible study. Another solid resource is the series *The Mysteries of the Bible* shown on A&E Television Network and available on DVD. The videos highlight scripture, provide background material, contemporary scholarship and disagreements among scholars, film footage, artwork, and commentary by noted and respected biblical scholars. Once you start looking, you will find abundant resources to enliven your Bible studies.

The use of the arts will enliven Bible study and help people to see the spiritual in everyday life. Their sensitivity to the sacred will be heightened and this awareness will enhance your Bible study times.

30

Make It Physical

I'm not advocating that your Bible study class become a gym-oriented group. Rather, I'm suggesting that body movement will illuminate and reinforce the texts being studied. For instance, if you are studying Exodus, you can do a couple of short movements to illustrate the lesson:

* After the Hebrews crossed the Sea of Reeds (Red Sea), Miriam led the people in a celebratory dance (see Exodus 15:20–21). Have some props available—tambourines, drums, musical sticks, ribbons, banners, and such. Set the context: a people who had been under oppression were suddenly free. As they fled, they were being chased by their oppressors. As they approached the Sea of Reeds, they knew it was over for them. But suddenly the sea parted and they were able to cross on dry land. As the last person reached the bank, the waters resumed their twirling and Pharaoh's army was drowned. The people were safe and free at last. Have the class join in the celebration by dancing as the text of Exodus 15 is read; they are to engage in a lively celebration of freedom. This can be great fun, although some may protest at first. If you have students with mobility issues, they can still find ways to join the celebration. Let them decide how much or how little they want to participate.

* A second activity illustrates the plight of the Hebrews' wilderness wandering (see Exodus 15:22ff). Have students walk around the room several times. If folks are able, have them carry their coats, hats, gloves, bags, and other items that might be in the room. Have them march around the

room again and again and again, until they have a sense of what it must have been like to trudge along without a clear destination. When I tried this with an adult Bible study, students thought it was funny and fun, at first. But the more we marched, the more frustrated they became. But they had a greater understanding of what the biblical folks encountered.

The aim is to get folks moving. This is not to turn the group into an aerobics class, but to make persons aware that they bring their whole selves to Bible study. Search out the various kinds of breath and body prayers to help folks center and focus on the lesson. The point is to engage the whole body in Bible study. Ask students for suggestions. They will have a lot, I'm sure.

③①

Let the Investigation Begin

Many people enjoy the hunt to solve a mystery. The popularity of such television shows as *Law & Order*, *CSI*, *Snapped*, *NCIS*, *The First 48 Hours*, and *Cold Case* lends credence to the statement that people love a puzzle. Why not use this to enhance Bible study? What if members of the class had a chance to "interview" a biblical character? While we know that's not possible in the "real world," anything is possible in the classroom.

This technique invites full participation by the class members. One approach is to divide the class into two groups. One group will represent the biblical character. The second group will represent the interviewer. This is a great way to engage students beyond the actual class time. They will figure out how to get together to complete the assignment. Or, if you wish, this can be an in-class exercise as long as you provide the necessary study aids to assist them.

Both groups will need to have some knowledge about the character and the action surrounding the character. This is an opportunity to provide information, or require the class to do the research to determine the context, the situation, and the character's role in the situation. The point is to have class members reach conclusions about how the biblical situation relates to their own lives or the wider community.

An essential aspect of this exercise is to allow students to come up with their own questions. Students will determine what questions to ask depending upon the approach they decide to take. In the face of incomplete information (this is generally true when dealing with the Bible), students will have to use their imaginations to fill in the blanks. Each question may lead to additional questions—all the better to help students really get into the biblical story. Students may protest that they don't know enough to be good at this. Pay them no mind. They will know more than they think they do and this is a chance for them to put their minds together in order to complete the assignment. It is not necessary, at first, to censor them; let them do their thing. More accuracy can be provided after the exercise.

Another approach is to focus on a particular issue or concern—say, a presidential election. The class can interview, for instance, Samuel, Saul, and David. These Israelite leaders can render opinions based on how they perform in the biblical text on various elements important to the election. How would David, a competent and charismatic leader, deal with immigration or taxation? How would Saul, a reluctant leader, deal with environment concerns and war? How would Samuel, a critic of leadership, advise Saul or David on health care and torture? The possibilities are endless and can be loads of fun.

Students should have time afterwards to debrief the experience, and the discussion should be lively. Begin the debriefing by asking some basic questions—what new did you learn about the biblical character? What insights did you gain about the biblical character as well as about yourself? What alternatives do these insights offer for contemporary situations that are similar? What role does God play in the human situation? Could there have been a different outcome? What would you have done in this situation?

32

I'm Asking the Questions Here!

The interview is an effective teaching method. The interview fosters class conversation and the personal involvement of the learner. This method can open up a text when the biblical character is the one being interviewed. Of course, we cannot travel back in time physically in order to question the character, so we have to use our imaginations. Another way of getting at the biblical text is for the learner to interview other church members or even family and friends. How do they view the biblical character or the biblical action? Their insights can help open up the text for the learner. Whether interviewing the biblical character or a real live person, the learner is sure to uncover something of value to enhance his or her own faith journey.

The Bible lends itself to the interview method; the men and women in the Bible become more real when we pose a series of questions to them. This will require students to read the text and think about what happens as well as what does not happen. It can be fun to assign characters to a group of learners and have them pose questions and answers. Their findings can be presented to the rest of the class. This method should generate different points of view and perspectives that spur lively conversations—among the particular group members and the class at large.

Some cautions: students may be hesitant to get into the spirit of the exercise. Assure them that there is no right or wrong way to uncover learnings. The interview may end up raising more questions than providing answers—and that's okay. The point is to gain some insight into the character as well as ourselves.

The characters we meet in the Bible are just like us in many respects—complex, layered, blends of good and not so good.

If you decide to use this method, it may be helpful to provide some starter questions for the students. A good place to start is with the basics: who, what, when, where, and how. Then, students can build on these basic questions by adding questions of their own. This becomes an opportunity for students to ask contemporary questions of ancient biblical characters. Be sure to caution that any "answers" that emerge will be interpretations since we cannot travel back in time to interview the biblical person. At the very least, students will come to understand how the Bible relates to the contemporary lives we are living now.

33

Wrestle with the Difficult Stuff

Some people want the Bible to be a ready and steady answer book. That is, whatever questions we have about the how's and why's of life, we expect the Bible to have an answer. The truth is that the Bible offers very few answers to the pressing questions of life. Even in the Psalms and prophetic books, questions abound: Why do the righteous suffer? Why do bad things happen to good people? Where do we go when we die? How can we know the mind and heart of God? Why do the wicked prosper? How does a loving God allow oppression and illness? The questions of theodicy abound. Theodicy, dealing with evil in the face of an all-knowing and all-loving God, is one among many Christian concepts that give us pause.

Rather than shy away from these concepts, provide a space for members to wrestle with them. In this setting, students bring their personal experiences to bear as they study the Bible. Also it's an opportunity to learn more about church history and how early church leaders dealt with the existential questions of life.

There are some books of the Bible that especially lend themselves to this kind of wrestling: Genesis, Job, Ecclesiastes, all the prophetic books, the Gospels, and the Book of Revelation. Of course, you will find complex theological grapplings throughout the Bible.

It is important to dig in and explore rather than gloss over or try to provide easy answers. The world in which we live is complex and getting more so each day. National and international decisions benefit some and harm some. What is the stance of believers in a world of rapid change? Are we to stand by and let the choices that are most expedient prevail? What can we expect if we raise our voices and pool our resources toward an alternative solution?

These are the kinds of questions with which Christians are called to deal. Again, creating a safe space is essential in order for people to voice their honest and candid feelings and thoughts. The point is not necessarily to create consensus, but rather to get people thinking about who they are and how they are to function in the world. Don't shy away from the hard stuff. There are blessings to be had by taking on the weightier things of the Bible.

34

Use the GPS or Map It Out

One of the tools for effective Bible study is a good set of maps. Maps do more than just show roads and rivers and mountains. Bible atlases also include information about the people who inhabit various areas, their main source of income (farming, metalworking, herding, etc.), the plants and vegetation that grow in the area, climate and seasonal changes. Many atlases include modern maps to show how land divisions changed over time.

Maps also show trade routes and the evolution of economic systems. In addition, we can learn about political events and the rise and fall of empires. Maps will show the routes various persons took during their lives.

For instance, it is an interesting exercise to chart the course the Hebrews took from Egypt to Canaan. By having a sense of the terrain, we can imagine how arduous and scary the journey was for them. Charting the geography of Jesus' public ministry brings the Gospels alive. Following Paul's preaching and teaching circuit gives us some idea about the tasks of his ministry and why it was important to start churches in various places. By doing this, we understand how Christianity spread and why there is such diversity in the early churches.

A good set of maps brings the biblical story alive and can ignite your congregation's thirst for knowledge. All it takes is a GPS!

35

Communion and the Bible

Do a short-term Bible study on communion or the Lord's Supper (the Last Supper). It is the time of remembering and renewing our commitment to God through the sacrifice of Jesus and is an important element of congregational life.

When I was a pastor in Chicago, we celebrated communion every first Sunday with our Spanish-speaking congregation. At least once a year I would teach a four-week course on communion. Members found it helpful to review the history of communion in the Christian church and to learn how it is celebrated in other cultures.

I used some familiar passages of scripture to guide the discussion: Matthew 26:20–29, Mark 14:17–25, Luke 22:7–38, John 13:1–38. You may include other references to communion, shared meals, and such found in the Bible. I included the hymns we normally sang during communion in the monthly worship services: "Let Us Break Bread Together" (African American spiritual based on Acts 2:42), "Una Espiga" ("Sheaves of Summer," a Spanish hymn by Cesáreo Gabaraín), "Be Known to Us in Breaking Bread" (by Moravian poet James Montgomery) as well as various verses in English and Spanish.

The use of hymns for communion is a good opportunity to study the various ways that communion is celebrated across cultures. Have on hand examples of services offered by Spanish, Korean, Chinese, or Japanese churches. We commemorate communion with bread and wine or juice. What do other cultures used for the elements? This will bring communion to life in an atmosphere where diversity will be celebrated.

A Bible study based on the sacrament of communion also serves as reminder that we await Jesus' return when we all will gather at God's great banquet table. You may want to end the class by serving communion. Or you can offer an agape meal—fruits, crackers, cheeses, whatever you and the class decide on—and members of the class serve each other. The symbolic meal will include many elements of the communion service. Students have found this kind of closing ritual a meaningful way to close their study of communion.

36

Baptism and the Bible

Baptism is a sacrament of the church whereby persons are joined to the body of Christ, to the members of a particular congregation, and to members of the Christian faith throughout the ages. It is an outward sign of an inward grace. The rite of baptism provides an opportunity to revisit the tenets of the Christian faith. A Bible study dedicated to the rite of baptism is an opportunity for persons to remember their baptism and connect it with their current life of faith.

Before you develop the class, you will want to consult your denomination's materials on baptism, a parallel Gospel version (I recommend *Gospel Parallels: A Comparison of the Synoptic Gospels,* edited by Burton H. Throckmorton, Jr. [Nashville: Thomas Nelson Publishers, 1989]) and a concordance. Each will provide texts to be included in the study.

You can begin a Bible study on baptism with John the Baptist (Matt. 3:1–6, Mark 1:1–6, Luke 3:1–6), Jesus' own baptism (Matt. 3:13–17, Mark 1:9–11, Luke 3:21–22), and the continuing importance of baptism in Christian scripture (such as: John 3:22–24; Matt. 28:19–20; Acts 2:37–42, 8:9–40, 10:23–48, 16:11–34, 19:1–7; Rom. 6:1–14; 1 Cor. 1:10–17; Gal. 3:26–28; Col. 2:8–23; 1 Pet. 3:18–22, among others). Include in your course outline information from denominational resources. Also, provide ample opportunity for persons to talk about their own baptisms.

You may want to include appropriate hymns during the class, for example, "Take Me to the Water" (African American spiritual based on Acts 8:36–38 and 10:47–48), or "Baptized in Your Name Most Holy" (German hymn by Johann Rambach).

Ask class members to submit the hymns that they find most meaningful. Or invite your minister of music or choir director to make some recommendations and possibly lead the singing.

As a closing ritual, you may want to conduct a renewal of baptismal vows ceremony in which the vows taken at the time of baptism are recalled. Water is then sprinkled on the back of the hand or the wrist as a symbolic recalling of baptism. It is not another baptism but rather a time to remember one's commitment to God, Christ, the church, and community. Consult worship resources for possible ceremonies and adapt them to fit your class. If some members opt not to participate, find other ways to incorporate them into the ceremony.

37

The Lord's Prayer and the Bible

Many congregations recite the Lord's Prayer every Sunday but have never taken the time to study it. A lively Bible study can be built on these familiar verses of scripture. And the Lord's Prayer can be part of a larger conversation about prayer. Bible study can focus on particular prayers in the Bible as well as the class members' prayer lives (or lack thereof). A Bible study on prayer will incorporate scripture from the Hebrew and the Christian scriptures as well as nonbiblical sources.

Matthew and Luke offer one of the central prayers of Christianity: Matthew 6:9–13 and Luke 11:2–4. Begin by noticing the differences between the two: What is the context? Who is the intended audience? To what is the prayer a response? What happens after the prayer? Other questions will emerge; let students list their questions.

As students engage the prayer, they will have questions related to their own personal prayer lives. Encourage the conversation and advise students that there are no easy answers. Their concerns may center on unanswered prayers—an issue that plagues many of us. The larger discussion about prayer will bring up feelings that will be difficult to share. Let students know that whatever they feel is valid, even when there are no ready answers or solutions to the dilemmas they face with regard to prayer.

This is an opportunity to experience various kinds of prayer as expressions of spirituality. A Bible study will include exploration of worship and praise prayers, prayers of thanksgiving, prayers of confession, prayers of supplication, intercessory prayers, and meditative prayers. There are others and they should be included.

Here are two resources for you to consider using for a Bible study based on the Lord's Prayer:

- *Becoming Jesus' Prayer: Transforming Your Life through the Lord's Prayer* by Gregory V. Palmer, Cindy M. McCalmont, and Brian K. Milford (Cleveland: Pilgrim Press, 2006).
- *The Lord's Prayer: Jesus Teaches Us How to Pray* by Mary Lou Redding (Nashville: Upper Room, 2011).

A Bible study focused on prayer will ignite your congregation. A praying congregation is one that is in the process of transformation.

38

Act It Out

As a child I loved the game Charades. It requires teams of folks to act out a phrase without using words. Instead, others have to guess the answer through gestures and hand signals. The phrases are usually book, song, television show, or movie titles. There is usually a time limit and a team gets a score for each correct answer. The process of acting out the phrase and guessing the answer can make for great fun.

When I was in seminary, one of my New Testament professors required each student to act out various passages of the Gospel. I was hesitant at first because it seemed silly to pantomime in a graduate level course. In addition, I didn't know my classmates well and felt that they would judge me negatively. And I confess that I was such a serious student that I resented the requirement to be a so vulnerable (and sometimes a bit silly) in class. Alas, there was no way out of the assignment for me. I had to perform in order to get a grade. And thank goodness! Once I swallowed my pride and let the Spirit take over, I had a blast! I began to look forward to the exercise and it helped me bond with my classmates. After class and over coffee, we laughed with each other and brainstormed on how to improve our techniques for the next exercise.

Far from being a childish exercise, the acting out of the Bible helped us with our teaching and preaching. The rationale of the professors was that we should be able to convey the essence of the Gospel without words. Each exercise required the cooperation of classmates to help. I realized that we were engaging in a modified version of Charades. Who knew this would be an effective way to get a message across to others? This is also a good way to engage adults in Bible study and the technique can be used with children and youth.

It is important to get your adult students to overcome their shyness and insecurities by first creating a safe space for them to be silly. Secondly, this exercise works better if there is an established sense of community among the class members. Folks are more likely to participate if they trust that they will not be judged or ridiculed for their participation. By creating a nonthreatening atmosphere, you ensure fuller participation for people to be silly without being overly self-conscious. Reassure students that this is a learning opportunity and that they will not be judged on their performances. Then again, you may discover some latent thespians in the class!

Students will have to use their imaginations both in acting out and guessing the scenario. Again, a time of debriefing is in order once the exercise is completed. This particular technique is especially powerful using the parables of Jesus. There are, however, other situations in the Bible that lend themselves to pantomime and Charades. Students will bond over their attempts, and the session should end with gales of laughter or thoughtful conversation. This exercise can deepen the sense of community and connection within the class. This will spread to other areas of church life and ignite your congregation. They can learn and have fun with each other.

There are some things to keep in mind when introducing this method for Bible study:

- Encourage students to enlist the help of others in the class; it's better if you let them decide whom they want to enlist.
- Emphasize that there is no right or wrong approach—all are valid.
- Allow enough time for students to rehearse before they perform in front of the group; assign the passage a week or so before the performance.

- Schedule in enough time for discussion and analysis of the biblical situation being acted out.
- Make sure that everyone participates—the introverts as well as the extroverts—in relatively equal ways.

This technique is a great way to get people into a biblical story and working together. It's a win-win situation all around.

39

Invite Guest Speakers

You will keep students engaged in Bible study by inviting guests to share with your class. The guest can be a member of the church, a person who lives in the community, or a relative of a class member. Persons are usually happy to be asked and will gladly speak on a particular topic.

For example, I learned that interns preparing to be funeral home directors and morticians have to fulfill hours of community service. I invited an intern to speak to my Bible study class Saved, Sanctified and Filled with the Holy Spirit. The intern talked about his faith journey that led him into mortuary science. He shared that his best friend was hit by a car and killed when they were eight years old. The intern witnessed the accident and stated how traumatized he was by how his friend looked after the accident. When he went to the funeral home to view his friend, he was amazed at how well he looked. He decided at eight that he wanted to bring that kind of comfort to others whose loved ones suffered a traumatic death. He talked about remembering people after death and assisting families in moving through the difficult task of letting their loved ones go. He represented a calm presence in the midst of sorrow and loss—a role he relished as well as his developing skill in making people look good after death. His story was moving and his commitment to his craft was an inspiration to the class.

As you study the Gospels, you may want to invite any certified public accountants or persons who prepare tax returns to talk to the class about money. If you are studying the prophets, you may want to invite members of the congregation who played a role in the civil rights movement, or the women's liberation movement, or the gay rights movement—anyone who can speak from their experience as a way to illuminate the scripture will be a plus. Be creative and ask someone to lead your class for a session or two.

Take a Field Trip

It will help to take your class out into the world from time to time. Most areas offer some resource to enhance Bible study. If your city or town has an art museum or art galleries with exhibits related to the Bible or religions, call to set up a tour with a guide. Students will be excited to learn something new as well as having the adventure of taking a field trip together.

If you are studying the prophets, plan a trip to agencies that are feeding the hungry or providing shelter for the homeless. Better yet, if possible, have the class volunteer at the agency and use the experience to further Bible study. There is a difference between reading about feeding the hungry, clothing the naked, welcoming the stranger, and visiting the prisoner and actually rendering service to them. Your students will gain insight into their own mission and ministry and learn, firsthand, what the prophets were trying to get across to their fellow Israelites. Another possibility is to hold your class in a nursing home and invite the residents to join you for the study. You may be surprised at the insights and wisdom the residents have to share with your class members. Be sure to call ahead and set things up before you go.

When I was a seminary student, our professor, the late Rev. Hycel Taylor, took us to the Cook County Jail several times. Our "assignment" was to conduct a Bible study with the inmates. We were responsible for selecting songs, composing prayers, selecting Bible study text, and providing lessons on the text. We students helped to bring hope to the young men and women incarcerated. And it was eye-opening to see the conditions in which they lived. We were always surprised at how well we were received despite our inexperience and anxiety about having a relevant word for the inmates.

Consider getting out of your comfort zone and doing something different to make Bible study alive. Take advantage of opportunities to get out of the classroom and do something for someone else. This requires some planning but it is well worth the effort to see biblical principles and learnings come alive.

41

Artsy Crafty Time

I used to scorn arts and crafts—until I had to do them for a Christian Education class in seminary. I learned the value of putting my thoughts and questions into pieces of yarn, crayons, paper, and glue sticks. You don't have to be an artist to use this method. In fact, the more you let students use their imaginations, the better the results will be.

You will have to do a bit of planning, though. Find a space in the church (preferably in the same room that the Bible study is held)—a shelf or box will do. Begin to collect supplies: construction paper, poster boards of various sizes, scissors, glue sticks, buttons, beads, popsicle sticks, paper clips, coins, clay, markers, rulers, scraps of cloth, tape, crayons, yarn. Ask students to bring things that can be used for art projects. Begin saving magazines, old calendars, post cards, etc.

Then create a space for people to create works that signify a learning or a question. A popular project I assign: create a visual that expresses your spirituality. Students are forced to think concretely about their faith and how that faith is manifested in their lives. Allow time for students to think and then to create. At the end of the exercise, students are invited to share their visual. Almost any theme, question, or concept can be used to fire up the imagination. You will be amazed at the quality of work and thought students will give to this exercise.

If students are willing, set a time aside for them to display their creations at coffee hour after worship. The students should be available to answer any questions that might come up about their individual work. This can be a fun time for persons to share a bit of their faith journey with members of the congregation.

Don't think this is too childish for adults. They really get into it. Their imaginations and creativity soar. They will want to do this artsy-crafty stuff again and again.

Show and Tell: Story Hour

Everybody has a story. Some will think their stories are not very interesting or enlightening. Some will be too shy to share their stories openly and freely. We can connect to the Bible through stories. The Bible is filled with stories of men and women just like us. Some are stories dealing with the themes of our own lives: confusion, surprise, doubt, fear, arrogance, disappointments, disaster, illness, violence, family strife, mistakes, good intentions, unexpected outcomes, unfulfilled dreams, dashed hopes, unexplained acclaim, undeserved riches, emptiness, sorrow, loneliness, betrayal—these stories and more are found in the Bible.

After the class has had some time to bond, ask members to share some stories about their lives: happiest times, most challenging times, a particular triumph or victory, a moment of regret, defining moments. Choose one of the stories appropriate to the Bible study and explore. Before too long, you will have to place time limits on the storytelling. Once people get started, they will want to go on and on.

Another strategy is to choose the focus for the Bible study. Invite class members to interview their family, friends, or other church members to speak on the topic of the Bible study. For instance, if you are studying Exodus, themes include oppression, fear, freedom, faith, celebration, worship. Students are to ask others to share a story that speaks to the theme.

A tried and true strategy is to read passages of scripture and have students paraphrase the story. This can be an individual or group exercise. At the end of an allotted period, students are invited to share their stories.

43

Plan a Memorial Service

Death is part of the life cycle. As one preacher put it, we are dying from the moment we take our first breath. So planning a memorial service is not an attempt to be morbid; rather it is an opportunity to celebrate a life. And we can learn a lot by the kind of service we develop for biblical characters.

There are texts that describe how persons died and give us glimpses into their funerals and memorial services. For example, see Genesis 50's description of the last days of Jacob and Joseph; and 2 Kings 9's description of Jezebel's demise.

Choose the biblical characters you want to memorialize and plan a service. You may want to consult your denomination for orders of service and resources or you can let students plan the service. At the very least, the memorial service should include the following elements:

- A site for the service: Will the service be in a house of worship? At a funeral home? At the deceased's home? In a forest? By a body of water? Will there be a portrait of the deceased? Will there be flowers? Will there be a printed order of service? Think about what the deceased would have liked.
- An officiant: Who will preside over the service? A rabbi, minister, or imam? A family member or friend? Who will be responsible for seeing that the service proceeds with dignity?
- Scripture and other readings: What speaks to the life of the deceased? You may want to include psalms, poetry, and other appropriate nonbiblical readings.

- Prayers: prayers are offered for the deceased and for the gathered assembly. Will you compose original prayers or use a prayer resource?
- An obituary: write an overview of the deceased's life—where the deceased grew up and lived, important achievements, contributions to the community, awards and recognitions, memberships in clubs or organizations, when the person died, and family members who are left to mourn the death.
- Music: choose the hymns and any special music that will set the tone and mood for the service; consult hymns and find interesting music on the Internet.
- The eulogy: the eulogy is the prepared presentation about the deceased as well as an invitation for the gathered assembly to think about their lives. Who will deliver the eulogy? Will music be playing softly in the background? Will the eulogy be more like a sermon or homily? Make it meaningful.
- Select persons to give tributes: invite family and friends to offer short tributes that give a window into the deceased's life and character. Tributes are personal stories that show appreciation for the deceased and can be comforting to the mourners gathered for the service.

Based on the topic of your Bible study, try including a memorial service. It will be interesting to see what your students will say about Eve, Adam, Samuel, Jeremiah, Malachi, Amos, Mary the Mother of Jesus, Judas, Pilate, Paul, Peter, Jesus. This is an opportunity to think more deeply about the lives of our biblical ancestors and our own lives.

Prepare a Roast

A roast is a public celebration of a person that is characterized by tributes, funny stories, insults, and affirmations given by family, friends, colleagues, and acquaintances. The roast is intended to be fun and good-natured rather than mean and vicious. At the same time, the roast should lift up positive attributes of the one being roasted. There is a master of ceremonies who keeps the event moving.

Bible study is a great venue for a roast. Choose a biblical character and determine who will give a roast. These can be other biblical characters or members of the class themselves. The point is to highlight some characteristics of the roastee, and it should be fun.

You may want to have characters outside the assigned text provide a roast. For instance, if Abraham is the roastee, you might want to highlight his unquestioning faith in God as well as his human attempts to sidestep danger. Roasters might include: Sarah, Hagar, Ishmael, Isaac, Lot, Pharaoh; and to mix it up even more, invite characters from the past and future to participate. What would Eve say about Abraham? Or David? Or Judas?

If Jacob is the roastee, you will want to highlight that he is a "mama's boy" in competition with Esau. Roasters will include Rebekah, Esau, Leah, Rachel, and Isaac, as well as Cain and the elder brother from the Prodigal Son parable. Again, let your imagination soar as you roast your favorite biblical characters!

Who's on Trial?

The aim of this method is to put biblical characters in conversation with each other, especially when they do not do so in the text. Most of us are familiar with courtroom scenes—in the news and as reality television. If not, watch a few episodes of the popular shows *Judge Judy, Judge Mathis, Judge Joe Brown, Judge Alex,* or *The People's Court.* It will only take a few shows to give you what you need to create a trial for Bible study. We know the major players: judge, defendant, defense attorney, prosecuting attorney, jury, witnesses, bailiff, and court recorder. There may be others but these tend to be the indispensable components of the courtroom. This method requires the class to create a mock trial with a particular biblical character as the defendant.

Students will need to be sufficiently familiar with the biblical text in order to render realistic portrayals of the characters. Divide the group into component parts and allow enough time for them to review the biblical text and their positions for the trial. Each "person" is the result of the collective wisdom of the group. That is, the defendant has to be clear about why he or she made the choices that put him or her on trial. The defense attorney has to have a clear plan for arguing the innocence of the client; the prosecuting attorney has to be clear why the defendant is guilty. Both will need to have questions for the various witnesses; the jury has to keep an open mind and base their verdict on the "facts" presented in the case. The judge's role is to keep the action moving.

This exercise is designed to explore the following questions:

◆ Who are the characters in the story?
◆ What is happening in the story?

- What is the challenge or conflict presented in the story?
- Who speaks and who is silent? Why?
- What does the story make us think or feel?
- How is the challenge resolved?
- What do we learn from the story?

I have used this method with teenagers and adults. They all get totally involved in the action of the trial. It's been amusing to watch students become the roles they are playing. It helps that the biblical character on trial raises credibility issues for us in the twentieth century.

Some likely candidates to stand trial are:

- Eve, accused of sparking the downfall of humanity; witnesses include the serpent, Adam, God, the tree of the knowledge of good and evil, the tree of life;
- Cain, accused of first-degree murder; witnesses include Eve and Adam, Abel's ghost, the ground that holds Abel's blood, God;
- Rebekah, accused of showing favoritism to an unscrupulous son; witnesses include Abraham and Sarah, Isaac, Jacob, Esau, God;
- Lot's wife, accused of looking back and committing suicide; witnesses include Sarah, Lot, angels, her daughters, a salt harvester, the mayor of Zoar, God, friends from Sodom and Gomorrah;
- Jezebel, accused of crimes against the state in the execution of Naboth; witnesses include Elijah, God, the prophets of Baal, Naboth's ghost, elders of Jezreel, and Jehu;
- Samson, accused of treason: witnesses include Mr. and Mrs. Manoah, first wife from Timnah, the men of Timnah, the ghosts of the men murdered at Ashkelon, Delilah, and God;

- The accusers of the woman caught in adultery, accused of attempted murder and slander; witnesses include Jesus, the woman, the woman's best friend, an elder in the crowd.

This list is not exhaustive, and the possibilities are abundant. Choose almost any characters, think about their "crimes," and place them on trial. Your students will have fun enacting court scenes. Allow time at the end of the trial to debrief the experience and explore learnings from the exercise.

Another approach is to have biblical characters sue each other. For instance, Eve sues Adam for defamation of character. Elijah sues Jezebel for reckless homicide in killing the prophets of God. Jezebel countersues Elijah for the deaths of Baal's prophets. Judas sues the disciples for slander and ruining his reputation. These pairings can be fun, interesting, and enlightening. Try it and see what happens!

46

State Your Case

The case study traditionally is used in business, medical, law, social science, and life science classes as a problem-solving approach to learning. A situation or problem is presented, facts and other bits of information are gathered about the case, and students reach a conclusion. The case study is a handy tool for congregational studies as well as Bible studies. The case study method entails viewing a problem or situation from a holistic standpoint—the who, what, when, where, and how. The case study should include people, places, events, decisions, policies, institutions. This makes it perfect for Bible study. The point of the case study method is to discern what in the text is applicable to contemporary life.

In Bible study, the "case" can be action focused or character focused. Students devise a system by which to explore the facts, assumptions, and outcomes of the case. The case can be a written piece that students are asked to dissect and then to reach conclusions about based on the content of the case. Or the case can be a project in which students gather the facts to put together a case and conclusion based on field research and then to present verbally to the rest of the class.

Cases can be written and given to students to complete. Or students can create their own case studies. Based on biblical texts and additional information from commentaries, dictionaries, and other resources, students can create a case study: What can we know about the character or action? What conclusion can we reach based on the evidence? For instance, one can analyze the character of Rebekah (Gen. 25–27) by exploring what she does, why she does what she does, what the outcome of her choices is, and what we can deduce about her based on the text. How does her story reflect a contemporary issue or concern? What is true about her story, and what lessons can we glean from her story?

Or students can be asked to create a case study based on the creation story found in Genesis 1–2. Students should name the characters in the text, including God; state the action as given; determine motivations; state the outcome; and explain what conclusions they reach about the text. Students may consult only biblical resources or use the case as an opportunity to interview members of the congregation or their family and friends. The point is that they pile together all the pieces to reach a conclusion.

The basic components of the case study should include the following:

- What characters make up the text?
- What is the background story for the text?
- What is the relationship among the characters?
- Are there cultural, social, economic, or political factors to consider?
- What is the conflict or point of tension in the text?
- How is the conflict or tension resolved?
- Who "wins" and who "loses"?
- What is the truth exposed by the text?
- What is the solution to the problem or tension?
- How does the solution connect to contemporary life? That is, what have we learned by exploring the case?

The case study approach can ignite your congregation because it invites people to share their thinking, to collaborate in the learning process, and to connect the Bible with real life.

47

Work with Key Words

Christians, along with Jews and Muslims, are called "people of the Book." That is, a support for our faith is the Bible, a book of words. And these words hold meaning and point us to the reality of God. These words also point to complex and confusing meanings. Words shape and inform how we see the world, each other, and ourselves. Words are important! A Bible study based on key words and phrases can yield great rewards.

You can create Bible studies that focus on particular words and concepts. Word studies will take your class through the Hebrew Bible (Old Testament) and the Christian Scripture (New Testament), and you will see how words and their meanings change over time and according to emerging contexts.

Students may be surprised to learn, for instance, that some words in the Bible are borrowed from secular settings and given theological meaning. Some words are borrowed from other cultures and given a distinctly Israelite meaning.

Consult a concordance and Bible dictionary to begin a list of words to study. You will want to consult commentaries to get a sense of how the selected words have been understood and how their meanings have evolved as the world has changed.

Some words you may want to explore are: covenant, blessing, curse, redeemer, exile, sin, steadfast love, fear, wisdom, salvation, justice, forgiveness, joy, righteousness, holy, repent, peace, law, light, bread, shepherd, vine. Again, this list provides some suggestions and is not meant to be exhaustive.

After you have selected the words for your Bible study, do some background work by consulting theological dictionaries of the Bible, such as the multivolume *Theological Dictionary of the*

Old Testament, edited by G. Johannes Botterweck and Helmer Ringgren (Grand Rapids: Eerdmans, 2003) and the one-volume *Theological Dictionary of the New Testament,* edited by Gerhard Kittel and Gerhard Friedrich and translated by Geoffrey W. Bromiley (Grand Rapids: Eerdmans, 1995). These volumes are lexicons that discuss Hebrew and Greek words, respectively, on an evolving theological level. Each will give scriptural references indicating where the word appears and the nuances in meaning. These lexicons are accessible to the average reader and help to illuminate the words in their scriptural context.

The word study lifts up theological concepts and challenges students to read the Bible with an eye towards deeper meanings. The stories they encounter in scripture will take on different meanings by their study of key words. This approach can be intimidating at first. Students will become more comfortable as the study continues. They will begin making connections among the words as well as how those words are used in church and life. They will learn how Israel gives new meaning to everyday words used in commerce, law, and other aspects of life.

Words are important. Bible study based on key words will open up conversations about faith and life by challenging people to be more precise with their choice of words.

48

Themes and Patterns

Here the possibilities are endless. The focus is on specific Bible study books. These are books with a particular theme based in scripture and complete with reflection and discussion questions.

There is a growing list of woman-focused Bible study books. A few authors and titles include:

- Athalya Brenner: *I Am . . . Biblical Women Tell Their Own Stories* (2005)
- Nicole Wilkinson Duran: *Having Men for Dinner: Biblical Women's Deadly Banquets* (2006)
- Barbara J. Essex: *Bad Girls of the Bible: Exploring Women of Questionable Virtue* (1999); *More Bad Girls of the Bible* (2009)
- Joyce Hollyday: *Clothed with the Sun: Biblical Women, Social Justice, and Us* (1994)
- Linda H. Hollies: *Jesus and Those Bodacious Women: Life Lessons from One Sister to Another* (2007); *Beloved, You Can Win: Strategies for Walking Your Talk* (2008)
- Vashti Murphy McKenzie: *Swapping Housewives: Rachel and Jacob and Leah* (2007)
- Helen Bruch Pearson: *Do What You Have the Power to Do: Studies of Six New Testament Women* (1992)
- Bonnie Thurston: *Women in the New Testament: Questions and Commentary* (1998)

Some highlight the seasons of the church year:

- Eugene Blair: *What Kind of Man Is Joseph and What Kind of Man Are You?* (2009)
- James A. Harnish: *Radical Renovation: Living the Cross-Shaped Life: A Lenten Study for Adults* (2007)

- Pamela C. Hawkins: *Simply Wait: Cultivating Stillness in the Season of Advent* (2007); *The Awkward Season: Prayers for Lent* (2009); *Behold! Cultivating Attentiveness in the Season of Advent* (2011)
- Cheryl Kirk-Duggan: *Mary Had a Baby: An Advent Study Based on African American Spirituals* (2003)
- Blair Gilmer Meeks: *Expecting the Unexpected: An Advent Devotional Guide* (2006)
- Beth A. Richardson: *The Uncluttered Heart: Making Room for God during Advent and Christmas* (2009)
- Donna Schaper: *Calmly Plotting the Resurrection: Lenten Reflections for Individuals and Groups* (2008)
- Don C. Skinner: *A Passage through Sacred History: Lenten Reflections for Individuals and Groups* (1997)
- Stillspeaking Writers Group: *Give It Up! Lenten Devotional 2012*

Others focus on prayer, discipleship, stewardship, faith, character—a search will reveal a multitude of titles. Your task will be to select those books that will be most helpful for your students. Also, ask around. Many people have books that they have found helpful.

49

Things We Wish Jesus Had Not Said

Jesus has a way of asking the deep question and challenging us to think about who we are and what we should be doing with our lives. And there are some things he said and asked that I wish were not in the Bible. This approach will certainly get people talking. I suspect we all have a list of things we wish could be avoided.

The following list is designed to get you thinking; it is not exhaustive. Your list may be very different from mine. That's fine. Use the list to develop a Bible study course that will keep folks coming week after week!

- "Why are you afraid, you of little faith?" (Matt. 8:23–27).
- "Do not think that I have come to bring peace to the earth; I have not come to bring peace, but a sword" (Matt. 10:34–36).
- "Who do the people say that the Son of Man is? . . . But who do you say that I am?" (Matt. 16:13–20).
- "For you always have the poor with you, but you will not always have me" (Matt. 26:6–13).
- "If any want to become my followers, let them deny themselves and take up their cross and follow me. For those who want to save their life will lose it, and those who lose their life for my sake, and for the sake of the gospel, will save it. For what will it profit them to gain the whole world and forfeit their life?" (Mark 8:31–9:1).
- "No slave can serve two masters; for a slave will either hate the one and love the other, or be devoted to the one and despise the other. You cannot serve God and wealth (Luke 16:1–13).

Think about the passages that give you pause; let them be the focus of a Bible study on the things we wish Jesus had not said.

50

Use Technology

Way back in the day, technology meant something very different than it does today. The use of cassette tapes was innovative for its time. With the appearance of VCRs and VHS tapes, we thought we had reached the apex of teaching methodology.

Today, these innovations are archaic and obsolete. Today, we have DVDs and Blu-Ray discs—and even these are met with some nostalgia. Technology changes so quickly we can hardly keep up. But consider using some aspects of it in your teaching.

PowerPoint presentations are growing in popularity and even the most technophobic can master the basics of the program rather quickly. Use the Internet for source materials and materials that enhance Bible study.

YouTube is a free video-sharing website where users can upload, share, and watch videos. Visit *www.youtube.com* to browse the offerings—movie excerpts, television clips, music videos, how-to videos, original short videos, and amateur videos. Visitors to the site can opt to register, which allows unlimited uploads.

Social networking services are abundant on the Internet. The most popular for general use is *Facebook,* a free social utility that allows people to connect. Users must register and are allowed to create a profile page, invite others to join, and send messages. In addition, you are able to create fan pages and group pages organized by various categories. Why not create a group page for your Bible study? You and others can post notes, messages, alerts, and links to other websites and articles, and you can continue conversations that originated in the class itself.

Google Groups is a free service that allows discussion groups. Users take part in threaded conversations through the website or via e-mail. Members are able to post comments, similar to bulletin boards, newsgroups, and Internet forums.

Blogs, or web logs, are personal online journals and usually focus on a particular subject. Many blogs are interactive and allow readers to post comments and send messages. In this sense, blogs are part of the social networking world. Many blogs feature text, images, music, videos, and links to other blogs and websites. A number of blog hosts charge a fee but you can set up a blog for free. Check out the following sites:

- www.thoughts.com
- www.wordpress.com
- www.livejournal.com
- www.insanejournal.com
- www.blogger.com
- www.tumblr.com
- www.weebly.com
- www.experienceproject.com

Twitter is a free online social networking service that allows users to send and read text posts up to 140 characters called tweets. In a sense, it is a micro blog site used primarily for updates; users can add links to other sites. The distinguishing feature of Twitter is the following/follower component. Many use Twitter to follow celebrities but it is gaining popularity as a networking tool.

New social networking sites appear daily. Ask around to determine the best site for your Bible study class.

Projects for Small Groups

Okay, again I must confess. I used to hate small group activities. It was so much easier for me to work on my own—no attitudes to deal with, no slackers to resent, and whatever grade I earned was based solely on my work. So I had no use for small group activities. All through undergraduate school, I tolerated small group projects and I never liked them. When I started seminary, I breathed a sigh of relief because surely there would be no small group stuff there. Right? Wrong! Throughout my seminary years, I was forced to work in small groups. It didn't matter the class—Bible, history, ethics, pastoral care—they all involved small groups at some point. I finally gave in and embraced small groups. And now I love them. Yes, tides can turn quickly.

You may encounter some resistance to project assignments. Some people don't like relying on others to get things done. There is always someone in the group who frustrates the others. Members sometimes will struggle over how best to divide the assignment responsibilities. But project work is a good way to foster cooperation in learning. People remember more when they engage in hands-on activities. There is learning in the doing as well as in the transmission of information.

The project can be approached from a number of ways. A simple project will be to research and report findings to the larger group; this approach is a good way to have students participate in Bible study. Another approach is writing a group report based on interviews or surveys of a particular passage, subject, theme, or character. Yet another approach is to have students follow up on a service or missional project. For instance, the Sisters in the Spirit group at Mt. Zion Congregational Church in Cleveland includes a service project at the end of the year.

It usually consists of collecting items to be donated to various agencies or organizations.

The project method brings people together and provides an experiential component to Bible study. The outcome is two pronged: learnings gained through the process of completing the project, and the end result or learning of the project. For instance, say that the theme is death: How does the Bible portray death? Where in the Bible are death scenes described? What are some common themes? How does your congregation deal with death? Who can be interviewed about this touchy subject? What kinds of questions should be posed?

Or students could report on what may have actually happened at the Last Supper. Based on the various accounts in the Gospels, students could reenact the scenario. They could interview other church members about what they think happened. The debriefing would include conclusions reached by scholars as well as how the events are depicted in popular culture.

In my comparative religion classes, I had students work in small groups to create utopian societies. They had to decide how to define utopia, break the society down into various parts (education, health care, military, housing, attitudes, etc.), and provide a visual presentation to the rest of the class. The presentations varied; some were simple while others were quite elaborate—posters, musical productions, PowerPoint slides, guest speakers, food indigenous to the society they created, costumes illustrating the ways people in the society dressed, codes of ethics, state constitutions, handbook for tourists—again, the possibilities are limitless. Students presenting the project were engaged and the audience was engaged so they could ask follow-up questions and seek greater clarification.

Students were required to meet outside of class times to work on the projects. However, I provided some class time for them to consult with each other and give updates on their progress.

The final step in this method is the debriefing and evaluation. Ask students what they discovered about the biblical text and about themselves. This method requires that a sense of community be established beforehand. This should result in candid and open conversation. Let students make recommendations for the next class to engage this method. Their learnings will help the instructor tweak the technique to fit your particular congregation.

The Bible as Literature

This Bible study approach focuses on the character development, plot, setting, and deeper meanings of biblical texts. We pay attention to themes, motifs (repeated elements), and imagery found in the texts. Such an approach gets at the lessons we can take away from studying scripture. We learn something about God and the human condition. We find in the Bible all sorts of people with various experiences making decisions that lead to conclusions about life.

Studying the Bible as literature forces us to ask basic questions: What is the text about? Who are the players in the text? What are they doing? Why are they behaving in the ways they do? What is the conflict or tension in the text? How is the conflict resolved? Who determines the outcome? Are there any surprises in the text? What are the lessons the text points to?

Many passages in the Bible can be read as story. As we have stated before, the Bible is a story writ large. It is the story of God and God's dealings with humanity. Here is an opportunity to read and study the Bible against the backdrop of our very lives.

A Closing Word

We live in a day and age where we are bombarded by words from a lot of different places. The words of faith are broadcast by those with loud voices, and their words are not always helpful. Words that castigate and condemn people because they do not conform to the "right" way of thinking are not helpful words.

As Christians we need to reclaim the words that have been distorted and twisted for narrow self-interest. Ours is the task to reclaim the scripture with integrity and a quest for truth. We begin this journey with Bible study. We are to engage the Bible from a faith stance and with a critical eye. We are challenged to understand the original settings of scripture and to wrestle with what the scripture can mean for us in the twenty-first century in the various settings and contexts in which we live and work.

In this volume, *52 Ways to Ignite Your Congregation . . . Bible Study*, I've tried to do a few things. First, I want you to start somewhere. Find a way to start Bible studies in your congregation. Find ways to support current Bible studies in your congregation. Find ways to create new Bible studies in your congregation. Bible study should be part of an overall faith formation plan. Education is all important to support our faith and understanding of what it means to be Christian in this day and age.

My second task was to provide some tips that will make starting and maintaining Bible study classes easier. Bible study leadership requires some planning and upfront investments. It is not sufficient to show up with a Bible and talk off the top of your head. I challenge you to invest as much time in preparing for Bible study as you do in preparing sermons. We ministers have a responsibility to provide ample study times for members of our congregation. We are the ones to train members to be leaders and teachers. It requires time, commitment, and preparation. These investments will pay off in an energized congregation with members eager to learn and embody their learning with increased church participation and involvement.

My third task was to open up some possibilities about how Bible study can look. Studying the Bible should not be drudgery. Instead, it should be fun and stimulating. Bible study can be a grand adventure, a leap of faith, and an opportunity to break out of ways of thinking that hinder and suppress. Bible study should be liberating and life-giving.

I hope I have achieved my goals. I leave you with these thoughts. The Bible is our book, the book of and about our faith. It is the story about God and God's dealings with us. It is a book that we approach through and with faith, but this does not mean that we cannot ask critical questions. We must. And we must understand that asking questions does not take away from our faith nor does it indicate that our faith is inauthentic. By seriously studying the Bible, we begin to see who God is, who we are, and the ways in which we move toward God and away from God. By seriously studying the Bible, we understand more deeply that God is about love, unity, justice, and community. By seriously studying the Bible, we encounter a God who offers unconditional love, a Christ who invites us to follow him, and a Holy Spirit who empowers us to be all that God has created us to be. By seriously studying the Bible, we come to realize that we have power and strength to overcome the anxiety, alienation, isolation, and loneliness that plague us. By seriously studying the Bible, we are assured that we are not alone in the world—we are in partnership and relationship with the One who is Alpha and Omega, the beginning and end, the author and finisher of our faith. Thanks be to God!

Resources/Bibliography

Alter, Robert. *The Art of Biblical Narrative*. Jackson, Tenn.: Basic Books, 1981.

Blair, Christine Eaton. *The Art of Teaching the Bible: A Practical Guide for Adults*. Louisville: Geneva Press, 2001.

Borg, Marcus J. *Meeting Jesus Again for the First Time: The Historical Jesus and the Heart of Contemporary Faith*. San Francisco: Harper-SanFrancisco, 1994.

Brown, Michael Joseph. *What They Don't Tell You: A Survivor's Guide to Biblical Studies*. Louisville: Westminster John Knox Press, 2000.

Bruce, Barbara A. *7 Ways of Teaching the Bible to Adults: Using Our Multiple Intelligences to Build Faith*. Nashville: Abingdon Press, 2000.

Bruce, F. F. *Hard Sayings of Jesus*. Downers Grove, Ill.: InterVarsity Press, 1983.

Brueggemann, Walter. *The Bible Makes Sense*. Louisville: Westminster John Knox Press, 2001.

Cooper, Joan. *Guided Meditation and the Teaching of Jesus*. Tilsbury Wiltshire: Element Books, 1982.

Essex, Barbara J. *Bad Boys of the Bible: Exploring Men of Questionable Virtue*. Cleveland: Pilgrim Press, 2002.

————. *Bad Boys of the New Testament: Exploring Men of Questionable Virtue*. Cleveland: Pilgrim Press, 2005.

————. *Bad Girls of the Bible: Exploring Women of Questionable Virtue*. Cleveland: Pilgrim Press, 1999.

————. *Bible for Vital Congregations*. Cleveland: Pilgrim Press, 2008.

————. *Bold and Brazen: Exploring Biblical Prophets*. Cleveland: Pilgrim Press, 2010.

————. *Misbehavin' Monarchs: Exploring Biblical Rulers of Questionable Character*. Cleveland: Pilgrim Press, 2006.

————. *More Bad Girls of the Bible*. Cleveland: Pilgrim Press, 2009.

Fokkelman, Jan. *Reading Biblical Narrative: An Introductory Guide*. Translated by Ineke Smit. Louisville: Westminster John Knox Press, 1999.

Furnish, Dorothy Jean. *Exploring the Bible with Children*. Nashville: Abingdon Press, 1975.

Hendricks, Obery M., Jr. *The Universe Bends toward Justice: Radical Reflections on the Bible, the Church, and the Body Politic*. Maryknoll, N.Y.: Orbis Books, 2011.

Henrich, Sarah S. *Great Themes of the Bible*. Volume 2. Louisville: Westminster John Knox Press, 2007.

Herzog, William R., II. *Parables as Subversive Speech: Jesus as Pedagogue of the Oppressed*. Louisville: Westminster John Knox Press, 1994.

Horsley, Richard A. editor. *In the Shadow of Empire: Reclaiming the Bible as a History of Faithful Resistance*. Louisville: Westminster John Knox Press, 2008.

March, W. Eugene. *Great Themes of the Bible*. Volume 1. Louisville: Westminster John Knox Press, 2007.

McEntire, Mark. *The Blood of Abel: The Violent Plot in the Hebrew Bible*. Macon, Ga.: Mercer University Press, 1999.

Niditch, Susan. *A Prelude to Biblical Folklore: Underdogs and Tricksters*. Urbana: University of Illinois Press, 2000.

Reid, Stephen Breck. *Listening In: A Multicultural Reading of the Psalms*. Nashville: Abingdon Press, 1997.

Robinson, Anthony B. *What's Theology Got to Do with It? Convictions, Vitality, and the Church*. Herndon, Va.: Alban Institute, 2006.

Seymour, Jack L., editor. *Mapping Christian Education: Approaches to Congregational Learning*. Nashville: Abingdon Press, 1997.

Smith, Sally Stevens. *Voices from the Story*. Bloomington, Ind.: Trafford Publishing, 2011.

Turner, Mary Donovan. *Old Testament Words: Reflections for Preaching*. St. Louis: Chalice Press, 2003.